Masterpiece recipes of

Athe merican club®

First edition.
Second printing, 1996.

Library of Congress Catalog Number: 93-77171

ISBN: 0-9635933-0-7

For additional copies of this book contact:

The American Club
Highland Drive
Kohler, Wisconsin 53044

Printed in USA by
Palmer Publications, Inc.
Amherst, WI 54406

Contents

Acknowledgements

This collection of recipes was prepared with the cooperation of the entire culinary staff of the Kohler Hospitality and Real Estate group. As you will read, there are nine different restaurants within this group, located in the village of Kohler, Wisconsin. The widely varying cuisines and menu themes of these restaurants offered a challenge in weaving together a recipe book that was representative of this diversity, yet cohesive in presentation. Our guests have come to savor the range of culinary options that sets the Kohler resort destination apart.

Very special thanks for bringing this recipe book project together goes to:

Rhys Lewis, Executive Chef of The American Club, for his direction, creative culinary guidance, contagious enthusiasm and overall talent in formulating the recipe book and marshalling it through the various kitchens.

Connie Giese, for testing each recipe. Her understanding of commercial kitchen operations combined with her knowledge of home kitchen techniques (along with her unfailing good humor) made it supremely easy for the chefs to work with her, ensuring that the recipes in this book have the taste of our kitchens and can actually be done at home!

Richard Palm, Pastry Chef of The American Club, for the sweet inspiration and crowning achievement his desserts provide to all our menus.

Doug Steiber, whose artful interpretations as Head Baker remind us daily why bread alone can be nirvana.

Aina Henegar, Manager of River Wildlife, and her inspired staff, who have created a mecca for gourmets and gourmands out of a wilderness retreat. They continue to enchant the palate with extraordinary creations.

Don Gruenke, who brought flair to golf clubhouse food. His restaurant would be a destination even without the championship golf that has made Blackwolf Run famous.

Mary Niemuth, for showing us that spa food can be splendid indeed.

Rene Bruggink, for her immeasurable help in collating recipe material, and her myriad behind-the-scenes efforts that kept the project "cooking."

Grace Howaniec, for her editorial consultation that helped our chefs sort the selection of recipes into an appealing collection for this book.

Rich Maciejewski and John Harvey, who accepted the challenge of capturing the flavors of our foods on film, and who, working only with talented (and obviously energetic) stylist LouAnn McCutcheon, managed an almost incomprehensible feat of shooting ten scrumptuous food photos in just two eight-hour days.

Edward Allmann, for diligently bringing together the talents of many creative people and steering the project to completion in its final hour.

Tom van Duursen, Director - Food and Beverage of The American Club, for his encouragement and expertise.

Alice Hubbard, General Manager of The American Club and Blackwolf Run, for shepherding the project, and keeping it (and everyone) from boiling over or being underdone.

Susan P. Green, Group Vice President - Hospitality and Real Estate, Kohler Co., for shaping The American Club into a place of culinary distinction.

Photo credits:
Image Studios, Appleton, Wis., front cover (food); p. 63 (bottom); p. 70 (top); p. 136.
John Harvey, Kohler Co., p. 65; p. 66 (bottom); p. 140.
Rich Maciejewski, Kohler Co., p. 63 (top); p. 64; p. 66 (top); p. 67 (top); p. 68; p. 69; p. 70 (bottom); p. 135; p. 137; p. 138; p. 139; p. 141; p. 142.

Masterpiece Recipes

of

THE AMERICAN CLUB

A Taste of History ❧ SCENT MEMORY. The fragrances recalled from home and childhood, from holiday feasts and anniversary celebrations — breads, cakes and fruit pies baking, soups and stews simmering, meat and fowl slowly roasting, and coffee brewing. This savory bouquet made THE AMERICAN CLUB an immediately familiar place to its early residents. When constructed in 1918, THE AMERICAN CLUB was intended to serve as a residence hall for "single men of modest means," primarily immigrants from northern Europe. For these early tenants, the reassuring smells of home-style cooking that drifted through THE AMERICAN CLUB's dormitory corridors made the transition to a new life in a new world a little easier.

❧

AS THE IMMIGRANTS ARRIVED ON THE WESTERN SHORE OF LAKE Michigan, leaving their families behind until they could find a permanent job and permanent housing, there was a growing need for "hygenic" temporary housing. Walter Kohler, the founder's third son and president of Kohler Co., conceived a residence hall that would serve not only as a domicile but would encourage the Americanization of its inhabitants. He explained his concept in the building's dedication speech in June, 1918:

> *"The name American Club was decided upon as it was thought that with high standards of living and clean, healthful recreation it would be a factor in inculcating in the men of foreign antecedents a love for their adopted country ... If this Club, besides providing suitable living conditions, be also an influence in the Americanization of the foreign born, and serve as a stimulus for greater love of country and a desire for a higher citizenship then its purpose will have been achieved."*

THE AMERICAN CLUB was the finest in habitat for Kohler workers. Within its walls was not just room and board, but an environment that nurtured the workers' hunger for

a better lifestyle and self-improvement. Walter Kohler felt that his workers deserved "... not only wages but roses as well," and THE AMERICAN CLUB was a brick-solid testament to that belief.

Within this new residence, huge kitchens prepared quantities of hearty fare to feed the hungry men. Robust portions of meat and potatoes based on recipes from the homeland were served. Hefty platters moved in caravan fashion from THE AMERICAN CLUB's kitchens to

Thanksgiving

FORTUNATE THE MAN WHO HAD THE PRIVILEGE OF EATING HIS THANKSGIVING DINNER AT THE AMERICAN CLUB THIS YEAR. THE FOOD WAS THE VERY BEST, SPLENDIDLY COOKED, AND SERVED IN THE MOST TASTEFUL MANNER. IT WOULD BE UNKIND TO THOSE WHO DID NOT HAVE THE OPPORTUNITY OF SITTING DOWN TO THIS FINE MEAL, TO PRINT THE MENU HERE. BUT IT WILL SUFFICE TO SAY THAT THE EASIER THING WOULD BE TO TELL THE THINGS THAT WERE NOT SERVED. NOW WE ARE ALL READY FOR THE CHRISTMAS DINNER, WHICH IS SURE TO BE A WONDER.

—from Kohler of Kohler News,
December, 1918

the waiting tables in the dining hall that is now The Wisconsin Room. No man went hungry. A news report from the period described the scene: "The tables fairly groan under the loads of wholesome food and the men can eat as much as they wish. There is only one rule in the dining room; that is to clean the plate. The manager wants nothing wasted."

We can only have a small sense of the sights and sounds of that time: An old photograph of the dining hall with oblong tables and benches end to end; a newspaper account of a Christmas menu served to the men. Imagine THE AMERICAN CLUB in those days: Scores of men, a symphony of dialects from Austria, Germany, Holland, Scandinavia, Russia — it was a cultural kaleidoscope. There was the clamor of the tap room (now the Horse & Plow), with evenings spent sharing exaggerated tales of the past, dreams of the future, and news of the day.

There was the sound of wooden pins crashing the bowling alley, an incongruous image since the space is now occupied by the gourmet Immigrant Restaurant, and bursts of laughter from dedicated players of skat and sheepshead. There was also the tranquillity of reading lounges where fireplace, player-piano and Victrola offered diversions (these areas, the Lincoln and Washington Rooms, are still peaceful retreats). In this con-

vivial   setting, the fraternity of these men was established on a common goal of hard work, fair pay, and self-improvement in America.

The north wing was added to The American Club in 1925 to provide more sleeping rooms and the pub. For the next half-century, The American Club continued serving both employees and residents of Kohler as the hub of community life.

A Dinner for 25¢

"Certainly the most popular room in the club was the dining room. Massive oak tables could accommodate as many as 300 for dinner. No one left hungry. At a typical meal, diners consumed 150 pounds of meat, five bushels of potatoes, 50 loaves of bread, 11 pounds of butter, 13 gallons of canned tomatoes, 9 pounds of coffee, 11 pounds of sugar ... and more. Workers paid 25¢ for meals during the week. The Sunday dinner cost 50¢. The increase was acceptable because, as one worker put it, "We can eat longer on Sundays!"

—remarks by Herbert V. Kohler, Jr. at
The American Club's 75th Anniversary Ceremony
July, 1993

*T*N 1978, THE AMERICAN CLUB WAS PLACED ON THE NATIONAL REGISTER OF Historic Places. By this time, the stately building had outlived its purpose and now stood at the heart of the community it had nourished with empty rooms and dim dusty halls. It

was then that an ambitious plan was initiated by Herbert V. Kohler, Jr., grandson of the founder of Kohler Co., to turn the aging tenant home for factory workers into one of the world's most lovely resort hotels.

The transformation proceeded with great caution to ensure the historical integrity of the place was respected. No bricks were altered. The finest in woods, textiles, and tile were crafted. Cultural values and the heritage of the past were married with modern conveniences to evolve an epitome of hospitality and a current definition of a home for gracious living.

Just as 75 years ago the needs and wants of the immigrant workers were so satisfied by the caring tenant residence hall, today THE AMERICAN CLUB is a functioning tribute to the pursuit of a more gracious life. That vision is now acknowledged with a host of awards that places THE AMERICAN CLUB within the elite of resorts worldwide.

There is a reverence for heritage, a preservation of certain values. It's in the way that

traditions are kept by Sue Green, Group Vice President of Hospitality and Real Estate, like the annual Sousa concert that recreates for today's generations the thrill of that afternoon long ago when the March King's baton led the Kohler village band on THE AMERICAN CLUB'S front lawn.

It's in the way that the gardens and lawns are artfully designed and maintained by John Green, Director-Kohler Landscape with collections of native prairie plants or elaborate

English formal gardens — carrying on the genius of village land planners and landscape architects which included the Olmsted Bros. known for New York City's Central Park and Harvard University's campus, Franz Lipp, and Vern Swaback of the Frank Lloyd Wright Foundation.

It's also in the way the land is regarded. You can sense the respect for it when walking the fairways of Blackwolf Run. When Pete Dye eyed the parcel that he would carve into 36 holes, the world-renowned course designer said there could not be a better natural setting for golf — and he kept it that way, natural. And it's in the way that a tranquil piece of wilderness beauty remains untouched nearby — River Wildlife wraps around the golf course and preserves for future generations the raw won-

der of land once known to Indian tribes as the best hunting and fishing grounds between Chicago and Green Bay.

There is no aspect of the resort environs today that does not speak to gracious living. Even the village market is a paragon and a paradox. After all, how many towns of 1,800 people can boast a gourmet 24-hour grocery with a New York- style deli, fresh fish flown in from across the continent, and its own brand of Kohler Farms Pure Lean beef. But Woodlake Market thrives. So, too, does Sports Core, in the pursuit of healthy lives. Fitness in spa surroundings has never been more appealing.

The luxurious AMERICAN CLUB resort hotel of today is different in many respects from the American Club residence hall of 1918. But for all that has changed, so much remains unaltered.

Back then, THE AMERICAN CLUB was one-of-a-kind. Today it still is.

The Restaurants

of

$\mathscr{L}$OOKING BACK OVER ITS HISTORY, THE AMERICAN CLUB HAS ALWAYS been known for its food. The first chef, Fritz Klutz, a Lithuanian immigrant, insisted on quality as well as quantity. Today's executive chef, Rhys Lewis, grandson of Welsh and German immigrants, is a master of delicate flavors, texture, and presentation. Issuing this collection of recipes is, therefore, most appropriate in celebration of the 75th anniversary.

The recipes that follow are favorites of THE AMERICAN CLUB guests and of the renowned chefs of the resort's restaurants. They represent the standard of good taste and creative use of ingredients that has made THE AMERICAN CLUB a destination for those who celebrate life and gracious living. What a delicious way to enjoy.

Standing left to right: Douglas Stieber – Head Baker, The American Club; Don Gruenke – Blackwolf Run Chef; Richard Palm – Pastry Chef, The American Club. Seated left to right: Connie Giese – Recipe Consultant; Rhys Lewis – Executive Chef, The American Club; Rene Bruggink, Mary Niemuth – Lean Bean Kitchen Supervisor.

The Immigrant

Immigrants still live in the memory of The American Club. A significant memento of their history is preserved in our most formal restaurant, The Immigrant. Six rooms of England, France, Scandinavia, Holland and Germany salute the heritage of those who left their

homes to venture to America decades ago. Dining here will exceed your highest expectation.

The Wisconsin Room

This great room at The American Club has heard it all, and in so many different tongues. The oak panels still retain the distant echoes of the thousands of meals that have been served here. This room was always invited to life's great occasions and is as much a symbol of the hotel's history as is the facade silhouette of peaked gables and green slate roofs.

The Horse & Plow

THE AMERICAN CLUB's Horse & Plow offers a robust fare. Food is hearty and filling — our version of the plates that graced so many well-scrubbed pine farmhouse tables of the past. Recalling its "tap room" origins, the Horse & Plow features a world tour of breweries with a dozen lagers and ales on tap and more than a score of others by bottle, too. Just as early AMERICAN CLUB residents called for their "tulips," you can still order a "yard" of beer here. And like those times when local beers were favored, you can also sample the product of select Wisconsin micro-breweries for a rare taste treat.

The Greenhouse

The great manors and hotels of Europe have a tradition of pausing after the entree. As if to separate two different experiences, dessert is delayed. THE AMERICAN CLUB accommodates that custom with the Greenhouse — a radiant place of stained glass splendor. A cloistered walkway leads you there, within the courtyard gardens, to this secluded dessert retreat.

River Wildlife

River Wildlife is a token of recogni-
tion that some lands should be unspoiled
and respected just for what they are.
River Wildlife is many things, but for
those with an adventurous culinary spirit
it is home. River Wildlife takes tradition
and adds to it a totally different perspec-
tive. Take from the wild its untamed
bounty presented with an unforgettable
flair.

RIVER
WILDLIFE
Kohler, Wisconsin 53044

Blackwolf Run

Blackwolf Run extends a special invitation to a log and stone porch and veranda
dining. Looking down upon the winding Sheboygan River Valley where Indians found
their best hunting and fishing between Chicago and Green Bay, you needn't love golf
to love this place.

Blackwolf Run dining rooms have earned a special standing among the fine restaurants at Kohler, and not just because they oversee the activity on two 18-hole Pete Dye
championship golf courses. Some people actually prefer to come in winter, when the
massive fieldstone fireplace is roar-
ing and the only players on the
fairways are herds of
white tail deer.

BLACKWOLF
RUN

Cucina

The Italian penchant for never needing an occasion to celebrate is echoed in Cucina. Life here is a celebration. Dining at Cucina is an uncontrived "divertimento" — a revelation of the luscious earthy recipes of Italy.

Cucina
a great Italian restaurant

The Lean Bean

The Lean Bean Restaurant is situated at the heart of the health and fitness center called Sports Core. It celebrates wholesome foods and healthful preparations, yet its desserts allow that a well-rounded life is rewarded with occasional indulgence.

Each summer brings the pleasure of the Marine Bean. This dining raft floats on Wood Lake, with its umbrellas in full sail setting a course for delightful outdoor dining.

In winter, with its cozy fireplace glowing, the Lean Bean offers the appealing contrast of window views looking onto a Wood Lake ice-scape or a tropics-like indoor swimming pool.

the Lean bean restaurant

Atrium Cafe At Woodlake Market

It is a measure of the unique attraction of Woodlake Market, that one could consider its circular, skylit cafe a destination in itself. Surrounded by overflowing displays of fresh produce and bordered by the Market's New York-style deli, bakery, salad and hot food buffet, visiting the Atrium is like stopping at a European streetside cafe. Since the Market is open 24-hours, this little restaurant never sleeps.

WOODLAKE MARKET
KOHLER, WISCONSIN

Appetizers & Hors d'oeuvres

Smoked Tenderloin of Kohler PureLean™ Beef 3
with Grilled Zucchini and Crisp Onions

Carpaccio of Beef and Roasted Tomatoes 4
with Roasted Pepper Puree and Basil Pesto Sauces

Seared Walleye 5
with Papaya Relish and Mango Butter Sauce

Smoked Atlantic Salmon 6
with Dried Cherry Chutney and Chive Cream
Grilled Smoked Cheddar Cheese Brioche

Grilled Barbecue Shrimp 7

Grilled Shrimp Cocktail 8
with Cucumber, Tomato Relish and Horseradish Sour Cream

Rabbit Ravioli 9

Wisconsin Four Cheese Phyllo Cushions 10

Ravioli Fritti 11

Warm Potato Pancakes 12
with Smoked Salmon and Sour Cream

Smoked Tenderloin of Kohler PureLean™ Beef

with Grilled Zucchini and Crisp Onions

yield 2 dozen

Beef Marinade:
- 5 cups hickory chips
- 3 sprigs rosemary
- 3 sprigs fresh thyme
- 3 sprigs oregano
- 1 tablespoon paprika
- ½ teaspoon cayenne pepper
- ½ teaspoon white pepper
- ½ teaspoon finely ground black pepper
- 1 tablespoon sugar
- 1 teaspoon garlic salt
- 1 teaspoon kosher salt
- 1 cup peanut oil
- 2½ pounds Kohler PureLean™ Beef tenderloin or a high quality beef

Zucchini and Onions:
- 1 clove garlic, chopped
- ¼ cup minced chives
  - Salt to taste
  - Black pepper to taste
- ½ cup vegetable oil
- 2 medium zucchini
- 1 cup flour
- 2 tablespoons chili powder
- ¼ teaspoon white pepper
- 1 teaspoon salt
- 2 large Spanish onions
  - Vegetable oil

This cold appetizer blends wonderful smoked and spiced flavors as well as tender, smooth and crisp textures in its melange of ingredients. Guests at The American Club will recognize this as one of their favorite hors d'oeuvres from our resort receptions.

Soak hickory chips in water for 24 hours.

Remove stems from rosemary, thyme and oregano; chop herb leaves. In a medium bowl, combine herbs with paprika, cayenne pepper, white pepper, black pepper, sugar, garlic salt, kosher salt and oil.

Marinate beef tenderloin in this mixture for 24 hours.

Remove beef from marinade, shake off excess. On a preheated outdoor grill, place drained hickory chips on top of coals to produce smoke. Place tenderloin on grill; cover. Cook only to rare, or until 115-120 degrees internal temperature. Chill well, preferably overnight.

In a large bowl, combine garlic, chives, salt, pepper, and oil. Slice zucchini into 24 slices, ¼-inch thick. Toss zucchini in herb oil to coat. Grill zucchini on preheated outdoor grill until cooked, but still crisp. Keep warm.

In large bowl, combine flour, chili powder, pepper and salt. Slice onions ⅛-inch thick. Dredge onions in seasoned flour. Deep fry in oil until crisp.

Remove beef from refrigerator and thinly slice. Fold beef to fit zucchini slices. Garnish with crisp onions.

Carpaccio of Beef and Roasted Tomatoes

with Roasted Pepper Purée and Basil Pesto Sauces

yield 4 appetizer servings

Beef:
- 12 ounces beef tenderloin, silverskin removed
- ½ cup grated fresh Parmesan cheese
- ½ teaspoon cracked black pepper

Roasted Tomatoes:
- 6 plum tomatoes
- Salt to taste
- ⅛ teaspoon sugar
- 2 tablespoons olive oil

Pepper Purée:
- 2 large red bell peppers
- ¼ cup olive oil
- Salt to taste

Pesto:
- ⅓ pound fresh basil
- 1 anchovy fillet
- 1 teaspoon chopped fresh garlic
- ¼ cup olive oil

The color and flavor of roasted bell peppers is among our most popular tastes. Add to that, roasted tomatoes, pesto, and the robustness of raw beef, and you have an elegant addition to your cocktail party.

Place the beef in the freezer until it is firm, but not hard. Slice into 16 uniform paper-thin slices. Reserve in refrigerator until use.

Cut tomatoes in quarters lengthwise. Place the tomatoes on a cookie sheet and season with salt and sugar. Roast in a slow oven at 225-degrees for 40 minutes. Remove and let cool. Toss with olive oil and reserve.

To make pepper purée, cook the peppers over a gas flame or grill until the outside is black. Place in a sealed container and let stand 10 minutes. Peel the skin off and discard. Cut in half and remove and discard seeds. Chop the peppers into ½-inch pieces and place in blender. Blend smooth. Add olive oil and salt; blend.

For pesto, wash the basil and pat dry. Remove the stems and place leaves in a food processor. Add the anchovy fillet, garlic, and olive oil. Chop basil mixture until it becomes a smooth liquid; scrape the sides often. Set aside.

To serve, spoon roasted tomatoes in the center of a serving plate or platter. Arrange beef slices around roasted tomatoes. Drizzle the basil pesto and the roasted bell pepper puree over the beef. Top with cracked black pepper and grated Parmesan cheese.

Photo on page 136

Seared Walleye
with Papaya Relish and Mango Butter Sauce
yield 4 servings

Walleye:
- 4 walleye fillets (4 ounces each)
- 1 tablespoon Jamaican Jerk spice
- 1 teaspoon chopped fresh garlic
  Kosher salt to taste
  Black pepper to taste
- 2 teaspoons vegetable oil (divided)
- 1 cup diced baby bok choy, ¼-inch dice
- 1 cup diced shiitake mushrooms, ¼-inch dice
- 4 small bunches diakon sprouts, for garnish

Relish:
- 1 cup diced watermelon, ¼-inch dice
- 1 cup peeled, diced papaya, ¼-inch dice
- ½ cup peeled, diced pineapple, ¼-inch dice
- ½ cup red onion, ¼-inch dice
- 1 tablespoon lime juice
- ½ teaspoon chopped fresh garlic
- ½ teaspoon peeled, finely chopped ginger
  Kosher salt to taste

Butter Sauce:
- 2 teaspoons chopped fresh garlic
- 1 cup peeled, pitted, finely diced mango
- ½ cup chardonnay wine
- ¼ cup heavy whipping cream
- 8 tablespoons butter

Live a bit on the edge and pair Jamaican Jerk spice with Wisconsin walleye for a distinctive hot, spicy sweetness. Add the tropical coolness of the papaya relish and your palate may never settle for the mundane again.

Season walleye with Jamaican Jerk spice, garlic, salt, and pepper. Heat a 12-inch sauté pan to high heat. Add 1 teaspoon oil; sear walleye until medium brown and fish flakes with a fork. Remove and finish in oven, if necessary. Reserve.

In a separate 12-inch pan, sauté lightly bok choy and mushrooms in remaining oil.

To make relish, blend together watermelon, papaya, pineapple, red onion, lime juice, garlic, and ginger in a large bowl. Season with kosher salt and chill. Reserve.

For butter sauce, in a medium saucepan, over high heat, combine garlic, mango, and wine. Reduce liquid to ¼ cup. Add cream and bring to a boil. Whip in butter 1 tablespoon at a time over high heat; blend smooth in blender or food processor.

To serve, place one-quarter of the bok choy and mushrooms in the center of serving plate. Place one fillet on top. Spoon one-quarter of the relish at three points on the plate. Spoon butter sauce in between the relish. Garnish with a small bunch of diakon sprouts.

Photo on page 63

Smoked Atlantic Salmon
with Dried Cherry Chutney and Chive Cream Grilled Smoked Cheddar Cheese Brioche
yield 4 servings

12 ounces Atlantic Smoked
  Salmon, sliced wafer thin into
  12 uniform slices

Chive Cream:
  4 ounces cream cheese, softened
  1 tablespoon minced fresh
    chives
    Salt to taste
    Black pepper to taste

Chutney:
  ¼ cup dried cherries, diced*
  ¼ cup red bell peppers, diced*
  ¼ cup red onions, diced*
  ¼ cup mangoes, diced*
  1 cup cucumbers, peeled,
    seeded, diced*
  1 teaspoon julienne cut mint
  ½ teaspoon minced fresh garlic
  1 tablespoon mango chutney
    Salt to taste
    Black pepper to taste

Garnish:
  4 leaves red oak lettuce
  4 leaves green oak lettuce
  4 leaves Belgian Endive
  6 slices Smoked Cheddar Cheese
    Brioche (see recipe on page 22)

The Dried Cherry Chutney makes this a colorful appetizer that will set the stage for a superb beginning to your next gourmet meal.

In a medium bowl, blend the cream cheese, chives, salt, and pepper. Reserve a room temperature.

Combine dried cherries, peppers, onions, mangoes, cucumbers, mint, and garlic. Add chutney and season with salt and pepper. Let stand.

Wash the greens and shake off excess water. Reserve.

On a broiler or grill, toast the Smoked Cheddar Cheese Brioche and cut in half diagonally.

With a pastry bag, pipe the chive cream cheese evenly in the center of four plates. Arrange three slices of salmon on each plate. Make a bouquet of baby greens and stick them in the cream cheese to stand upright.

Spoon three teaspoons of the chutney on three points of the plate. Finish each salmon dish with three half slices of grilled Smoked Cheddar Cheese Brioche. Set brioche between salmon and chutney.

*Chef's Note: Dice dried cherries, red bell peppers, red onions, mangoes, and cucumbers into 1/4-inch pieces, holding knife diagonally to get a slanted cut.

Grilled Barbecue Shrimp

yield 4 servings

Mopping Sauce:
- ¼ cup strong coffee
- 1 tablespoon vegetable oil
- 1 teaspoon liquid smoke
- 1 teaspoon chili powder
- 1 teaspoon salt
- 1 teaspoon Worcestershire sauce
- 1 teaspoon packed brown sugar
- ¼ cup ketchup

Shrimp:
- 20 raw shrimp (13-15 count per pound)
- 1½ cups Firecracker Barbecue Sauce (see recipe on page 178)
- 8 bamboo skewers

Mopping sauce recipes are carefully guarded by their creators since the sweet flavor associated with barbecue depends on a tasty mopping medium. You'll enjoy the interesting flavor blend from our chef's recipe.

In a small stainless steel bowl, combine coffee, oil, liquid smoke, chili power, salt, Worcestershire sauce, brown sugar, and ketchup. Blend well; set aside.

Peel shrimp, cut along the back with a small knife to devein. Toss into the mopping sauce. Refrigerate for one hour. Drain shrimp.

Soak bamboo skewers in water for 30 minutes before use. This will prevent the skewers from burning.

Place five shrimp on a skewer and put a second skewer through shrimp to prevent the shrimp from spinning. Grill on a preheated hot grill 2-3 minutes on each side. Brush with barbecue sauce and serve hot.

Grilled Shrimp Cocktail
with Cucumber, Tomato Relish and Horseradish Sour Cream

yield 4 servings

Shrimp:

12 shrimp (13-15 count per pound), peeled, deveined, and tails removed
Salt to taste
Black pepper to taste
1 tablespoon stemmed, chopped fresh thyme
1 tablespoon vegetable oil
4 sprigs whole cilantro, for garnish

Relish:

1 lime
¼ cup peeled, seeded, cucumber, ¼-inch dice
¼ cup seeded tomato, ¼-inch dice
¼ cup peeled red onion, ¼-inch dice
Salt to taste
Black pepper to taste
1 tablespoon packed brown sugar
½ teaspoon chopped fresh cilantro

Sour Cream Sauce:

½ cup sour cream
1 tablespoon horseradish

Everyone loves shrimp as an appetizer but few serve it in interesting, novel presentations. This grilled shrimp with its colorful, fresh-flavored relish and zippy horseradish sour cream sauce will get attention—and requests for the recipe.

Season the shrimp with salt, pepper, and fresh thyme; coat with oil. Grill on hot grill until cooked fully but not tough. Reserve in refrigerator until use.

To make relish, squeeze juice from lime. (You should get ¼ cup.) In a medium bowl, combine cucumbers, tomatoes, onion, salt, pepper, brown sugar, lime juice, and cilantro. Gently blend; set aside.

In a small bowl, combine sour cream and horseradish; mix well and reserve.

To serve, arrange the shrimp in a pinwheel on serving plate or platter with the tails toward the center. Spoon some of the relish in the center of the shrimp. With a small spoon dot the sour cream next to each of the shrimp. Garnish with whole cilantro.

Rabbit Ravioli

yield fifty ravioli

Pasta:
- 2 cups semolina flour
- ½ cup all-purpose flour
- 1 tablespoon olive oil
- 3 large eggs
- 3 tablespoons water

Rabbit and Sauce:
- 2 rabbits (4 pounds each) cleaned, rinsed, patted dry, cut into serving pieces
- Salt to taste
- Black pepper to taste
- 2 tablespoons vegetable oil
- ⅔ cup diced carrot
- ⅓ cup diced celery
- 1 cup diced onion
- 1 cup brandy
- 1 cup burgundy wine
- 1 quart water
- 1½ teaspoons minced garlic
- 1 teaspoon oregano
- ½ teaspoon thyme
- 1½ cups diced tomatoes

Garnish:
- ½ pound wild mushrooms, cepes, shiitakes etc. sliced
- 2 tablespoons butter
- 1 large egg
- 1 tablespoon water
- 1 tomato, finely diced
- ¼ cup chopped fresh chives
- 2 tablespoons grated fresh Wisconsin Parmesan cheese

Tender homemade ravioli boast an Old World richness of flavors in a rabbit, wine and herb filling enhanced by wild mushrooms. This delightful departure from the Italian tradition is perfect for anyone with a discriminating and adventurous palate.

In a mixer with a dough hook, combine flours and oil; mix. Slowly add eggs and water until large pea-size balls appear. Roll up dough, wrap and let rest 1 hour.

Season rabbit well with salt and pepper. In a large dutch oven sear rabbit in hot oil. When brown, remove rabbit from pan and reserve. Add carrots, celery, onions; sauté. Add brandy, wine, water, garlic, oregano, thyme, and tomatoes. Place rabbit back in liquid and simmer for 1 hour or until tender. Remove rabbit from pan, chill in refrigerator. Continue to simmer liquid until it reduces to sauce consistency; strain and discard vegetables. Reserve sauce; keep warm.

Remove rabbit from refrigerator, pick meat from bones and chop rabbit meat very fine. Set aside.

In a large skillet, sauté mushrooms in butter. Add sautéed mushrooms to reserved sauce.

Roll dough out thin, approximately 1/16-inch. Cut with 4-inch round cutter.

Place rabbit meat on pasta circles, just off center. Beat egg and water together and brush edges of pasta with egg wash; fold in half.*

Place ravioli in a large pot of gently boiling water for 3-5 minutes or until done.

Arrange ravioli on a serving platter. Spoon sauce over ravioli and garnish with tomatoes, chives, and Parmesan.

*Chef's Note: The ravioli can be frozen and cooked as needed.

Wisconsin Four Cheese Phyllo Cushions

yield 4 servings

¼ cup finely grated Wisconsin Asiago cheese
¼ cup finely grated Wisconsin provolone cheese
¼ cup finely grated Wisconsin mozzarella cheese
½ cup finely grated Wisconsin Parmesan cheese (divided)
1 tablespoon coarse grain mustard
8 sheets phyllo dough, about 14 by 18-inches
½ pound butter, melted, cooled to lukewarm

Leave it to The American Club chefs to find a way to "rev" up a favorite recipe. Phyllo cushions are standard among appetizers, but this filling of aged provolone and Asiago cheeses combined with more typical mozzarella and Parmesan cheeses is not. The result speaks for itself.

In a medium bowl, blend together Asiago, provolone, mozzarella and ¼ cup of grated Parmesan. Add the mustard; mix to blend well.

Lay 1 sheet of the phyllo dough on a cutting board (keeping the rest covered with a damp cloth to avoid drying when not using). Brush some melted butter on the layer of dough and top with another layer of phyllo dough; repeat until you have four layers. Divide the dough lengthwise into approximately seven 2½-inch wide strips. Place 1 tablespoon of the cheese mixture onto each strip and turn dough down in the form of a triangle. Continue folding until the phyllo strip is used. Place the triangles on cookie sheet as they are made and brush the tops with butter and dust with Parmesan cheese. Repeat procedure with remaining 4 sheets of phyllo dough and cheese mixture.*

Bake in a preheated 350-degree oven for approximately 10-15 minutes until golden brown and serve immediately.

*Chef's Note: Can be made ahead and stored in refrigerator until time to bake.

Ravioli Fritti

yield 18 ravioli

1 recipe Italian Cheese Medley
   (see recipe on page 175)
1 recipe Marinara Sauce
   (see recipe on page 179)

Pasta:
2 cups semolina flour
½ cup all-purpose flour
1 tablespoon olive oil
4 large eggs (divided)
4 tablespoons water (divided)

Breading:
2 cups all purpose flour
3 large eggs, beaten
3 cups dry bread crumbs
   Vegetable oil

A great crowd pleaser—this tangy marinara sauce with homemade deep-fried ravioli is guaranteed to please people of all ages. You can count on guests wanting seconds.

Prepare Italian Cheese Medley recipe. Reserve in refrigerator.

Prepare Marinara Sauce recipe. Reserve in refrigerator.

In a mixer with a dough hook, combine flours and oil; mix. Slowly add 3 eggs and 3 tablespoons water until large pea-size balls appear. Roll up dough, wrap and let rest 1 hour. Roll out dough to a thin sheet, approximately $\frac{1}{16}$-inch thick. On half of dough, place 1 tablespoon of prepared cheese medley every 5 inches.

Beat together remaining egg and water to make egg wash. Brush between cheese medley with egg wash. Place other half of dough sheet on top. With a 2½-inch cutter, cut out ravioli circles. Press dough together on edges to seal. Chill, covered in refrigerator for at least 30 minutes.*

Remove ravioli from refrigerator. Use the triple breading procedure, with three bowls: one with flour, the second with beaten eggs, and the third with bread crumbs. Dip each ravioli starting with the flour and ending with bread crumbs.

In a skillet of hot oil, deep fry ravioli until golden brown. Serve with hot marinara sauce.

*Chef's Note: The ravioli can be made one day ahead. Can also be frozen.

Warm Potato Pancakes
with Smoked Salmon and Sour Cream
yield 1½ dozen pancakes

4 baking potatoes (10-12 ounces each), peeled
Salt to taste
Black pepper to taste
1 tablespoon lemon juice
1 large egg
1 tablespoon minced onion
2 tablespoons finely sliced chives (divided)
⅓ cup vegetable oil
8 ounces smoked salmon, sliced thin
½ cup sour cream
2 tablespoons Golden Great Lakes caviar

This simple appetizer is both pleasing to the eyes and the palate. You must taste this combination to believe how good it is.

In a medium bowl, shred the potatoes finely with a hand shredder or process in food processor. Season with salt and pepper. Add the lemon juice. Squeeze the potatoes to get rid of excess water. Set aside.

In a small bowl, combine egg, onions and 1 tablespoon chives. Add to potatoes, mix well. Divide the potatoes into 16 even balls. Pour half of the oil in a heavy bottomed sauté pan. Heat oil to medium heat. Add potato balls to sauté pan, flatten with spatula and cook until golden brown on both sides. Allow to cool to room temperature.

Portion the salmon into 16 even pieces. Roll and arrange each roll neatly on each potato pancake. Spoon a small amount of the sour cream on each salmon roll and garnish with the remaining 1 tablespoon chives. Spoon the golden caviar evenly on the sour cream and serve.

Breads & Baking Choices

The American Club's Signature Rye Bread

yield 2 loaves

1 teaspoon granulated sugar
2 packages (¼ ounce) active dry yeast
¼ cup warm water (105-115 degrees)
2 cups buttermilk (110 degrees)
½ cup honey
½ cup dark corn syrup
1½ teaspoons salt
2 teaspoons *ground* caraway seed
2 tablespoons unsweetened cocoa powder
1 cup rye meal, available in health food stores
2 cups medium rye flour
4 cups (approximately) bread flour

Hearty, hard-crusted rye breads are a tribute to a baker's skill. Ground caraway seed, unsweetened cocoa powder and a combination of rye meal and rye flour contribute to the complex flavors. This is the sandwich bread served in our Horse & Plow Restaurant.

In a small bowl, dissolve the sugar and yeast in the warm water. Let stand 5 minutes; allow to foam profusely.

In a separate large bowl, using an electric mixer or by hand, combine the warm buttermilk, honey, dark corn syrup, salt, *ground* caraway seed, and cocoa powder. Add the rye meal and mix thoroughly. Add the medium rye flour ½ cup at a time and mix thoroughly. Start adding the bread flour ½ cup at a time and stir to form a firm dough.

Remove dough from bowl, place on floured surface and cover it with dish towel. Let it rest for 10 minutes.

Knead the dough until smooth and elastic, about 12 minutes. Put dough in a large, greased bowl, turning once to coat dough. Cover with plastic wrap and a dish towel. Put in a warm (80-degree) place. Let rise until double in volume, about 2 hours.

Punch down and let rise again, until doubled in volume; approximately 2 more hours.

Punch down again and form into 2 round loaves. Put in two 9-inch greased round cake pans. Let rise until doubled.

Bake in a preheated 350-degree oven for 45 minutes to 1 hour or until done. Remove from pan and wrap in dish towels. Let cool on racks.

Swedish Limpa Rye Bread

yield 2 loaves

2 packages (¼ ounce each) active dry yeast
½ cup warm water (105-115 degrees)
1 teaspoon sugar
1½ cups warm milk (105-115 degrees)
1 teaspoon anise seed, crushed
1 teaspoon fennel seed, crushed
1 tablespoon orange zest, finely chopped
½ cup honey
2½ cups medium rye flour, divided
1½ teaspoons salt
5 tablespoons butter, melted (divided)
3½ cups (approximately) bread flour

A traditional sweet Swedish rye bread that blends the flavors of anise, fennel and orange in a complex taste that can easily become addictive. This bread is superb for sandwiches.

In a large mixing bowl, dissolve the yeast in the warm water. Add the 1 teaspoon sugar. Let stand 5 minutes to allow yeast to foam.

Add the milk, anise, fennel, orange zest, and honey. Mix with an electric mixer or by hand. Add 2 cups of the medium rye flour and salt. Mix very thoroughly; add 4 tablespoons melted butter and the remaining ½ cup medium rye flour. Mix in the bread flour ½ cup at a time until a stiff dough is formed.

Cover with a dish towel, and let rest for 10 minutes before kneading. Turn dough onto a floured surface and knead with the palms of your hands until smooth, about 10 minutes. Place dough in a lightly greased bowl. Turn over to grease top. Cover with plastic wrap and a dish towel. Place in a warm place to double in bulk, about 1 to 1½ hours.

Punch down dough. Divide dough into 2 equal pieces and shape each into a ball. Place smooth side up in two lightly greased 9-inch cake pans. Cover with a dish towel and let rise until double, approximately 45 minutes to 1 hour.

Bake in a preheated 375-degree oven for approximately 45 minutes or until brown. Remove bread from pans and place on cooling racks, brush with remaining 1 tablespoon butter while still hot. Cool completely, before serving.

Photo on page 67

Finnish Cardamom Bread

yield 2 loaves

1 package (¼ ounce) active dry yeast
¼ cup warm water (105-115 degrees)
¾ cup warm milk (105-115 degrees)
½ cup sugar
½ teaspoon salt
2 large eggs
1 teaspoon ground cardamom
4½ cups (approximately) all purpose flour, unsifted (divided)
½ cup butter, melted and cooled
⅓ cup pearl sugar*
⅓ cup blanched sliced almonds

For Egg Wash:
2 large eggs
1 tablespoon milk

A run-away best seller at our annual Holiday Market. No matter how fast the pastry staff baked these tender, fragrant loaves redolent of cardamom and studded with pearl sugar, they couldn't keep up with the demand. Make these loaves at home and try to save some slices for toast. It is heavenly!

Line a large cookie sheet with parchment paper or you may lightly grease the cookie sheet.

In a large mixing bowl, combine yeast and water. Let stand 5 minutes to soften.

With an electric mixer, blend in milk, sugar, salt, eggs, cardamom, and 2 cups of the flour. Beat until smooth. Then add melted butter and blend well. Stir in an additional 2¼ cups flour. Beat until thoroughly mixed.

Place dough on floured board and knead with the palms of your hands until dough is smooth and has a satin-like feel, approximately 10 minutes.

Place dough in a greased bowl and turn over to grease top. Cover and let sit in a warm (80-degree) place until doubled in volume, approximately 1½ to 2 hours.

Punch down dough, divide in half to form into two round loaves; about 8″ in diameter and 2″ high. Place on cookie sheet and let rise again until doubled in size.

To make egg wash, beat eggs and milk together. Just before baking loaves, brush with egg wash and sprinkle with pearl sugar and sliced almonds.

Photo on page 67

Bake in a preheated 350-degree oven for approximately 25 to 30 minutes or until golden brown.

Remove from oven. Take loaves off of the cookie sheet and place on cooling racks to cool completely.

*Chef's Note: Pearl sugar can be found in specialty food sections.

Onion Walnut Bread

yield 1 loaf

9 tablespoons chopped onions
3 tablespoons vegetable oil
3 cups bread flour
1½ tablespoons powdered nonfat
dry milk
¾ teaspoon sugar
1½ teaspoons salt
3 tablespoons walnuts, chopped
1½ tablespoons active dry yeast
1¼ cups minus 1 tablespoon
warm water (90 degrees)
2 teaspoons onion powder

Guests at Blackwolf Run Restaurant have always enjoyed this out-of-the-ordinary yeast bread. Try this in your own kitchen and savor this popular treat.

In a small frying pan, sauté onions in oil until transparent. Remove from heat; cool to room temperature.

In a large mixing bowl, with a dough hook or by hand, mix together bread flour, powdered nonfat dry milk, sugar, salt, walnuts, yeast, warm water, and onion powder. Add the sautéed onions and mix at medium speed until dough is formed, about 12 minutes.

Form dough into a ball. Place dough in a greased bowl, turning once to coat dough, cover with plastic wrap and a dish towel and let rise in a warm (80-degree) place until double in size, about 1½ hours.

Punch down dough; shape into a loaf. Put into lightly greased 9x5x3-inch pan. Let dough rise until dough is 1-inch above the pan rim.

Bake in a preheated 350-degree oven for approximately 45-55 minutes or until golden brown, remove from pan immediately. Let cool on wire rack.

Whole Wheat Walnut Bread

yield 3 loaves

2 packages (¼ ounce each) active
dry yeast
2½ cups warm water (105-115
degrees)
1 tablespoon honey
1 tablespoon packed brown
sugar
½ cup powdered nonfat dry milk
2 tablespoons butter, room
temperature
2 teaspoons salt
2 cups bread flour
4½ cups whole wheat flour
2½ cups walnut pieces
2 large eggs
1 tablespoon milk

A good, old-fashioned hearty bread that uses honey and brown sugar for its hint of sweetness. An abundance of walnut pieces enrich the flavor of this glazed yeast bread.

In a large bowl, dissolve yeast in warm water; blend in honey and brown sugar. Stir in dry milk, butter and salt.

Add bread flour mixing to blend. Add whole wheat flour ½ cup at a time until batter is thick and difficult to stir. Let batter rest 3-4 minutes while large flour particles absorb moisture. The dough will be sticky. Turn the ball of dough onto floured work surface and knead with the palm of your hand for 5 minutes.

Return dough to a greased bowl, turning once to coat dough and cover with plastic wrap and a dish towel. Leave at room temperature until doubled in bulk, 1 to 1¼ hours.

Place dough on work surface and flatten it. Put half the walnuts in the center and fold dough over nuts. Repeat with the balance of walnuts, folding dough until nuts are absorbed in dough.

Divide dough in 3 equal parts; shape each into a loaf. Place in greased 9x5x3-inch loaf pans.* Cover with wax paper and let rise in warm (80-degree) place for about 50 minutes.

Beat eggs and milk together to make glaze. Just before baking, brush loaves with egg milk glaze. Bake in a preheated 375-degree oven on middle shelf of oven for 40-50 minutes or until dark brown. Remove from pans immediately. Cool on wire rack.

*Chef's Note: Dough may be shaped into round loaves and baked on greased cookie sheets. Good to eat cool or toasted, and it freezes well.

Photo on page 67

Pumpkin Bread

yield 3 loaves

1 cup vegetable oil
3 cups sugar
4 large eggs
2½ cups canned pumpkin
1½ cups pecans, chopped
2¾ cups bread* flour
½ cup pastry* flour
1 teaspoon cinnamon
1 teaspoon baking powder
1½ teaspoons salt
1½ teaspoons nutmeg
2 teaspoons baking soda

Don't wait until autumn to bake this moist breakfast bread. It uses the convenience of canned pumpkin combined with pecans, cinnamon and nutmeg for its rich, fall-like flavors. This is a quick bread whose very essence says "welcome."

In a large mixing bowl with an electric mixer or by hand, combine oil and sugar. Add eggs, pumpkin and pecans.

In a separate large bowl, combine bread flour, pastry flour, cinnamon, baking powder, salt, nutmeg, and baking soda. Stir into sugar mixture until well blended.

Spoon mixture into greased and floured 9x5-inch loaf pans. Bake in a preheated 350-degree oven for approximately 50 minutes, or until a wooden pick inserted in center comes out clean. Cool bread in pans for 30 minutes, then remove and place on cooling racks until cool.

Bread freezes well.

*Chef's Note: Pillsbury Gold Medal does make a bread flour. Check with your grocer. Pastry flour is a soft wheat flour and can be found in a health food store.

Smoked Cheddar Cheese Brioche

yield 3 loaves

2 packages (¼ ounce each)
  active dry yeast
1¾ cups warm water (105-115
  degrees)
¼ cup sugar
5½ cups all-purpose flour
2 teaspoons salt
6 large eggs
1¼ cups butter, room
  temperature
4 ounces smoked cheddar
  cheese, shredded
1 large egg
1 tablespoon milk

Egg-rich, light and tender brioche just gets better with the inclusion of smoked cheddar cheese. Use this with our Smoked Salmon Appetizer as the Immigrant Restaurant does.

In a medium bowl, combine yeast, warm water and sugar and let stand for 5 minutes to proof the yeast, making sure the mixture foams profusely.

In a large mixing bowl, combine the flour and salt together. Stir in the yeast solution and the eggs. Mix in a powerful electric mixer, with a dough hook at medium speed until dough pulls cleanly away from the bowl. You will have to stop the mixer fairly frequently and scrape it down with a rubber spatula to achieve this result. This should take about 15 minutes. Add the softened butter gradually and continue to mix as before until the dough pulls cleanly away from the sides and the bottom of the bowl. Dough will be very elastic.

Place dough on unfloured surface. With both hands pull dough towards you, sprinkle half of the shredded cheddar cheese on the dough, flip the dough back over itself. Repeat process until all cheese is thoroughly incorporated.

Place dough in a lightly greased bowl and refrigerate, covered with plastic wrap, overnight.

Remove dough from refrigerator. Separate dough into golf ball size balls. Lightly grease 9x3-inch loaf pans. Stagger balls in loaf pan, each pan should hold 8 balls. Let dough rise in a very warm (90-degree) place, until doubled. (Top of your preheated oven would be best.)

Dough texture will resemble gelatin. Whisk together egg and milk for egg wash. Gently brush top of dough with egg wash.

Bake in a preheated 400-degree oven for approximately 45-50 minutes, until very dark brown and set. Immediately remove from pan and cool on cooling rack.

Pizza Dough

yield four 10-inch crusts

4 cups (approximately) flour
(divided)
½ teaspoon salt
½ teaspoon granulated garlic
1 package (¼ ounce) rapid rise
dry yeast
1¼ cups water (120 degrees)
1 tablespoon olive oil
1 tablespoon honey

Our Italian restaurant, Cucina, uses this hint-of-garlic dough for its superb, upscale pizzas. This is an easy, satisfying yeast dough for beginners in bread making. Use it as a base for any pizza toppings.

In a large mixing bowl combine 3½ cups flour, salt, garlic, and yeast.

In a small bowl mix together water, olive oil and honey. Add to flour mixture and mix with a heavy wooden spoon until it comes together into a ball.

Place dough on a floured surface and knead with the palm of your hand until a smooth dough is developed, approximately 7 minutes. Use remaining flour to knead dough if needed. Cover dough and let rest for 10 minutes at room temperature. Roll dough out into four 10-inch circles.* Place dough on pizza screen.

Prebake in a preheated 400-degree oven for 4 minutes. Top with desired toppings and bake at 400 degrees until done.

*Chef's Note: This can be made ahead of time. Divide dough into 4 equal parts; wrap in plastic wrap and freeze until use. Thaw under refrigeration before use.

Photo on page 67

Tips for Successful Baking

1) Always use liquids warmed to 105-115 degrees Fahrenheit.

2) To proof yeast, always dissolve the yeast in water. Allow the yeast to foam before using it.

3) *Never* put salt directly into the yeast liquid. Blend salt with flour first (flour buffers the salt). Salt hurts yeast action when alone.

4) Always mix batter well; avoid over kneading.

5) Add flour ½ cup at a time to avoid dry dough.

6) Let dough rise in warm (80-degree) place. Cover dough, don't let it dry out.

7) Let dough rise until almost doubled.

8) Always preheat oven.

9) Thoroughly bake the bread and test it. Don't just bake it until browned, sometimes this isn't enough. You may test with a toothpick.

10) If you like a soft crust, brush with melted butter or vegetable oil. For a chewy crust, wrap in tea towels. For harder crust, spray with water just as it enters the oven and just before it leaves the oven.

Soups

Smoked Onion and Black Bean Soup
with Three Tomato Salsa and Cumin Sour Cream
yield 12-14 servings

1 recipe Three Tomato Salsa (see recipe on page 172)

Soup:
- 3 cups dried black beans
- 6 cups cold water
- 1 cup hickory chips, soaked in water
- 2 cups sliced onion, ¼-inch thick
- ¼ cup vegetable oil
- 2 tablespoons peeled, chopped garlic
- 1 bay leaf
- 2 teaspoons chili powder
- 8 cups Chicken Stock (see recipe on page 184)
- Salt to taste
- Black pepper to taste
- 16 leaves fresh cilantro, for garnish

Sour Cream:
- 1½ cups sour cream
- 2 teaspoons ground cumin
- Salt to taste
- Black pepper to taste
- 1 tablespoon lime juice

If you haven't discovered the glorious flavor and color of black beans in recipes, begin your initiation with this spicy, robust soup that carries a hint of the Caribbean in every mouthful.

One day before assembly, prepare beans and onions. In a large mixing bowl, place black beans in 6 cups water and refrigerate overnight.

Also prepare onions by preheating an outdoor grill to medium high heat; place the soaked hickory chips on the coals and allow to generate smoke. Rub onions lightly with vegetable oil, just enough to coat. Reserve remaining oil. Place on grill, cover and smoke for 30 minutes. Remove onions from grill. When cool, chop into ¼-inch dice. Store in refrigerator overnight.

In a two-gallon soup pot, add the remaining oil, smoked onions, garlic, bay leaf, and chili powder. Cook 1-2 minutes and add the drained, black beans and chicken stock. Bring to a simmer and simmer for 1½ hours, stirring so the beans do not stick. When the beans are tender to the bite, they may be puréed or left whole. Season to taste with salt and pepper. Set aside. Remove bay leaf.

In a small bowl, combine sour cream, ground cumin, salt, pepper, and lime juice. Reserve in refrigerator until use.

To serve, ladle hot Black Bean Soup into serving bowls. Spoon a dollop of cumin sour cream on top and garnish with salsa and the cilantro leaves.

Five Onion & Wild Rice Soup

yield 12 servings

Roux:
- ¾ cup clarified butter*
- ½ cup flour

Soup:
- 1 cup julienne cut shallots
- ½ leek, julienne cut white part only
- ¾ cup julienne cut red onion
- ½ cup julienne cut Bermuda onion
- 1½ teaspoons vegetable oil
- ¼ cup cream sherry (divided)
- ½ gallon Chicken Stock (see recipe on page 184)
- 1½ quarts heavy whipping cream
- Salt to taste
- White pepper to taste
- ½ teaspoon cayenne pepper
- 1½ cups wild rice, cooked and drained
- 1 scallion, chopped, for garnish

A featured soup on our banquet menu, this soup recipe is frequently requested by our guests. It is relatively easy to make and your guests will probably ask for the recipe, too. If you like onions and cream soups, this one is especially for you.

To make clarified butter,* melt ¾ cup butter in small saucepan over low heat. When completely melted, remove from heat, let stand for about 5 minutes allowing the milk solids to settle to the bottom. Skim the foamy white butterfat from the top; discard. Spoon off the clear yellow liquid and reserve—this is the clarified butter. Set aside. Discard the milk solids on the bottom of the pan. You should have approximately ½ cup clarified butter for this recipe.

Whisk flour into clarified butter until well blended, and cook until roux becomes gold-colored. Set aside.

In a two gallon stock pot, sauté shallots, leek, red and Bermuda onions in oil. Add ⅛ cup cream sherry; simmer 5 minutes. Add chicken stock; bring to a boil, reduce heat and simmer 5-10 minutes. Add heavy cream; bring to a simmer. Whisk in roux slowly and thicken to proper consistency. Season with salt, white pepper and cayenne pepper. Add cooked rice and remaining ⅛ cup cream sherry.

Garnish with chopped scallions and serve piping hot.

Minestrone

yield 12-14 servings

1 cup dry white beans, soaked in water overnight
1 cup dry black beans, soaked in water overnight
Salt to taste
1 cup diced pancetta ham (Italian bacon)
1 pound cubed beef stew meat
4 cups diced onions
2 cups diced carrots
2 cups diced cabbage
½ cup chopped garlic
2 bay leaves
1 tablespoon dried leaf basil, crumbled
2 tablespoons chopped fresh thyme
2 teaspoons chopped fresh oregano
1 teaspoon black pepper
3 quarts Beef Stock (see recipe on page 183)
1½ cups tomato puree
3 cups diced tomatoes
1 cup frozen peas
1 cup frozen corn
3 cups cauliflower, stems removed, separated into florets
¼ pound fresh leaf spinach, washed, stemmed
Kosher salt to taste
¼ cup Basil Pesto (see recipe on page 171)
½ cup grated Wisconsin Parmesan cheese

Don't let the list of ingredients scare you away from making this classic Italian vegetable soup. It is well worth the effort. For maximum flavor, prepare this one day in advance of serving so that the flavors have time to blend.

In two medium saucepans, cook the white and black beans separately in salted water to cover. Cook until tender, but not overcooked, approximately 30 minutes. Remove from pan; drain and rinse well. Reserve.

In a 5-6 quart soup pot, cook pancetta until crispy. Remove from pan, reserve. Brown the beef in the fat from the pancetta.

Add onions, carrots and cabbage. Sauté on medium heat, until vegetables are translucent. Add garlic, bay leaves, basil, thyme, oregano, and pepper. Cook for 2 minutes.

Add beef stock, tomato puree and diced tomatoes. Bring to a simmer; cook for 20-30 minutes or until beef is tender. Add peas, corn, cauliflower and reserved cooked beans. Cook until vegetables are tender.

Remove bay leaves. Add leaf spinach at the end, so it maintains its fresh green appearance. Season to taste with kosher salt.

Just before serving, add the basil pesto and reserved pancetta. Sprinkle with Parmesan cheese.

Creamy Beef Stroganoff Soup

with Cracked Black Pepper Noodles

yield 12-14 servings

Soup:

- 5 cups cubed roast beef or tenderloin tips
- 4 cups Chicken Stock (see recipe on page 184) or chicken broth
- 4 cups Beef Stock (see recipe on page 183) or beef broth
- 1 tablespoon Worcestershire sauce
- 1 teaspoon ground black pepper
- 1 teaspoon ground celery seed
- 1 teaspon ground thyme Salt to taste
- 3 cups sliced fresh mushrooms
- 3 cups chopped onion
- 3 cups chopped celery
- 1 tablespoon chopped garlic
- 1 cup Marsala
- ½ cup dry white wine
- 6 cups heavy whipping cream
- 2 cups sour cream
- ½ cup flour
- ½ cup butter

Noodles:

- 1 cup plus 2 tablespoons flour Pinch salt
- 1 tablespoon cracked black pepper
- 2 large eggs
- 1 tablespoon cold water

Beef stroganoff fans take note! You can still recapture the lovely flavor and texture of the classic entree by making this hearty, rich soup. Complete the menu with hard-crusted bread and a crisp, green salad.

In a large skillet, over medium heat, brown beef on all sides. Remove from heat and reserve. In a large Dutch oven, bring chicken and beef stock to a boil. Add reserved beef, Worcestershire sauce, black pepper, celery seed, thyme, and salt. Simmer for 30 minutes. Add mushrooms, onions, celery and garlic. Simmer until vegetables are tender, appoximately 15 minutes. Add Marsala and white wine. Add heavy cream and sour cream, bringing to just below boiling point; stir constantly.

In a small saucepan melt butter. Stir in flour and bring to boil stirring as mixture thickens. Remove from heat. Whisk into soup mixture, stirring until thickened. Keep warm.

To make noodles, in a large bowl, combine flour, salt and pepper. Make a well in middle and add eggs and water. With a wooden spoon stir mixture to form a ball. Turn onto lightly floured surface and knead until smooth and elastic. Cover and let rest for 15 minutes. On floured surface with floured rolling pin, roll dough to 5x12-inch rectangle. Cut into ⅛-inch strips for medium noodles. Cut again to desired length.

In a 6-quart saucepan, heat 3 quarts of water to boiling point. Add noodles and bring to boil; remove from heat. Drain and rinse with cold water. Add cooked noodles to soup.

Great Lakes Smoked Chub Chowder

yield 12-14 servings

4 large baking potatoes
1 pound smoked chubs
2/3 cup plus 2 tablespoons butter (divided)
1 cup peeled, diced onion
4 teaspoons chopped garlic
1 bay leaf
3 sprigs finely chopped fresh thyme
1/2 gallon clam juice
2/3 cup flour
1 quart heavy whipping cream
Salt to taste
White pepper to taste
4 tablespoons finely chopped chives, for garnish
Leeks cut into thin strips, for garnish

A comforting "cousin" of clam chowder, this rich soup derives its splendid, smokey flavor from Great Lakes smoked chubs. This is a soup that makes a meal, along with a good green salad.

Peel and dice potatoes; boil in a small pot until tender. Do not overcook.

Peel and discard skin from chubs. Carefully debone, separate meat from bones, leaving meat in various sizes. Set aside.

Melt 2 tablespoons butter in a large soup pot and add onions, garlic, bay leaf and fresh thyme. Cook slowly, stirring to avoid burning. Add the clam juice and bring to boil; simmer gently for 10 minutes. Set aside.

To make a roux, in a small pot melt remaining 2/3 cup butter and stir in flour until smooth. Gradually whisk roux into soup until smooth. Simmer 5 to 10 minutes.

Add cream and the drained, cooked potatoes to the soup. Add the smoked fish to the soup. The fish will add salt to the soup so do not season the soup before adding the smoked fish. Taste for seasoning. Remove and discard bay leaf.

Garnish soup with chives and leeks.

Photo on page 63

Chicken Enchilada Soup

yield 8 servings

1 green bell pepper
3 jalapeno* peppers
1 medium onion
3 green onions
2 tablespoons vegetable oil
2¼ cups milk
2¼ cups water
1½ tablespoons chicken base
½ cup butter
1 cup flour
2 cans nacho cheese soup (10¾ ounce each)
½ teaspoon cumin
¾ teaspoon chili powder
1 jar pimentos (7 ounces), chopped
2 cups cooked, diced chicken
   Flour tortilla chips, for garnish

Who would have guessed that the ingredients in a Mexican staple would translate so nicely into a soup? The Lean Bean Restaurant chefs did—and created a soup that is a favorite of guests.

Seed and chop peppers; chop onions. In a medium skillet, sauté peppers and onions in vegetable oil. Sauté until tender/crisp. Remove from heat and reserve.

In a large soup pot, heat milk and water. Add chicken base.

In a large saucepan, melt butter and add flour to make a roux; stir until smooth. Add all hot milk mixture, ½ cup at a time, to roux; stir until smooth. Pour back into soup pot; stir constantly until thickened. Add nacho cheese soup, cumin and chili powder; stir. Add reserved peppers and onions; stir. Add pimento and chicken; stir and heat through.

To serve, garnish with flour tortilla chips.

*Chef's Note: When handling hot peppers, avoid touching face and eyes. Wash hands thoroughly with warm, soapy water; rinse well.

Cheddar Cabbage Soup
yield 12-14 servings

8 cups Chicken Stock (see recipe on page 184)
½ cup dry white wine
14 cups chopped cabbage
4 cups chopped onion
3 cups chopped celery
2 tablespoons lemon juice
1 tablespoon white wine Worcestershire sauce
2 teaspoons ground black pepper
2 teaspoons chopped garlic
1 teaspoon ground celery seed
½ teaspoon ground thyme
1 bay leaf
Salt to taste
8 cups heavy whipping cream
6 cups grated Wisconsin cheddar cheese
½ cup butter
½ cup flour

River Wildlife is renowned for its wonderful soups. This comforting blend of fresh green cabbage and Wisconsin cheddar cheese hits the spot after a day with Mother Nature.

In a large soup pot, bring chicken stock and wine to a boil. Add cabbage, onions, celery, lemon juice, Worcestershire sauce, black pepper, garlic, celery seed, thyme, bay leaf, and salt to taste. Bring to a boil; simmer until cabbage is tender, about 25 minutes. Add heavy cream and heat to just below boiling point. Slowly add cheddar cheese while stirring constantly.

In a small saucepan, melt butter; add flour to make a roux and mix until smooth. Whisk roux into soup and bring to a boil, stirring as it thickens. Remove bay leaf. Serve.

Wisconsin Three Cheese Soup

yield 12-14 servings

½ pound butter
2 cups diced onions
2 tablespoons chopped fresh garlic
½ cup flour
2 quarts milk
2 bay leaves
½ pound shredded Wisconsin jalapeno jack cheese
½ pound shredded Wisconsin cheddar cheese
½ pound shredded Wisconsin Swiss cheese
Salt to taste
Black pepper to taste
Dash nutmeg
12 ounces Wisconsin beer

We love cheeses in Wisconsin and this popular, creamy cheese-based soup is an example of our menus reflecting the state's agricultural richness. You can sample this tasty soup daily in our Horse & Plow Restaurant.

In a 1½ gallon soup pot, melt butter; sauté onions and garlic until tender. Add flour; mix well. Cook for 5 minutes, stirring frequently over medium heat. Add milk. Whip with a whisk to blend in milk. Add bay leaves. Cook over low heat for 20 minutes, stirring constantly.

Stir in cheeses, stirring in one direction only until thoroughly mixed and cheese is melted. Season with salt, pepper and nutmeg. Remove bay leaves. Stir in beer and serve.

Fire & Ice Soup
Hot Grilled Shrimp
with Chilled Gazpacho and Avocado Relish
yield 4 servings

Gazpacho:
- 1 **cup chopped green bell peppers**
- 1 **cup chopped plum tomatoes**
- 1½ **cups peeled, chopped cucumber**
- ½ **cup sliced scallions**
- ½ **cup diced Bermuda onion**
- 2 **teaspoons minced jalapeno* peppers, seeded**
- 1 **tablespoon peeled, chopped garlic**
- 1 **tablespoon freshly squeezed lemon juice**
- 2 **tablespoons freshly squeezed lime juice**
- 2½ **cups vegetable juice**
- 2 **teaspoons stemmed, chopped cilantro**
- 2 **teaspoons chili powder**
- ½ **teaspoon cumin**
- ½ **teaspoon salt**
- ½ **teaspoon black pepper**

Avocado Relish:
- 1 **cup peeled, seeded, diced avocado**
- ¼ **cup diced Bermuda onion**
- 1 **cup diced yellow bell pepper**
- ½ **teaspoon chopped garlic**
- ½ **teaspoon cumin**
- 1½ **teaspoons lemon juice**
- 1½ **teaspoons lime juice**
- 1 **teaspoon chopped, stemmed cilantro**
- 1 **teaspoon packed brown sugar**

This southwestern version of a classic cold Spanish soup is culinary innovation at its best. Spiced grilled shrimp is cooled by the icy, crispness of the gazpacho. If you are looking for a summer stunner—this is it!

In a large mixing bowl, combine peppers, tomatoes, cucumbers, scallions, onions, jalapeno peppers, and garlic. Process in blender or food processor and return to bowl. Add lemon juice, lime juice, vegetable juice, cilantro, chili powder, and cumin. Stir to mix well and refrigerate, covered, for 24 hours.

In a medium bowl, combine avocado, onion, pepper, garlic, cumin, lemon juice, lime juice, cilantro, and brown sugar. Mix gently; do not over mix. Set aside.

Preheat an outdoor grill to high heat.

Season shrimp with oil, salt, pepper, garlic, and garlic chili pepper sauce. Grill shrimp on a hot grill for 2 minutes on each side until opaque. Remove and reserve in a warm place.

To serve, remove gazpacho from refrigerator; season with salt and pepper to taste. Spoon gazpacho into four shallow bowls.* Arrange three shrimp in the center of the bowl in a pinwheel shape. Garnish the center of the shrimp with the avocado relish and serve.

Photo on page 64

Shrimp:
- 12 raw shrimp (16-20 count), peeled and deveined
- 1 tablespoon vegetable oil
- Salt to taste
- Black pepper to taste
- 1 teaspoon finely chopped garlic
- 1 tablespoon Thai garlic chili pepper sauce

*Chef's Note: When handling hot peppers, avoid touching face and eyes. Wash hands thoroughly with warm, soapy water; rinse well.

The remaining gazpacho soup can be frozen for later use.

Carrot and Dill Soup

yield 12-14 servings

3 pounds carrots
1 large onion
2 tablespoons butter
3 tablespoons peeled, diced shallots
1 tablespoon peeled, chopped garlic
1 bay leaf
1 tablespoon chopped fresh thyme
2 cups white wine
2½ quarts rich Chicken Stock (see recipe on page 184)
3 cups heavy whipping cream
Salt to taste
White pepper to taste
Sour cream, for garnish
Fresh chopped baby dill, for garnish

Carrots are often neglected in soups (except for an obligatory token amount) and that's a shame since their colorful sweetness is perfect in soups. Try this puréed, smooth and creamy soup in its picture-perfect presentation.

Peel and dice carrots and onion. Melt butter in large soup pot over medium heat. Sauté carrots, onions, shallots, garlic, bay leaf, and thyme. Deglaze with the white wine; reduce until liquid is nearly gone. Add the chicken stock and simmer until the carrots are tender. Add heavy cream, stirring to blend. Season to taste with salt and pepper. Remove bay leaf.

Pour soup into blender in batches and purée until smooth. Pass it through a sieve. Before serving, reheat slowly—do not boil.

Top with a dollop sour cream and sprinkle with dill; serve hot.

Five Herb Soup
with Wilted Spinach and Asiago Cheese
yield 8 servings

2 tablespoons butter
2 cups onions, ¼-inch dice
1 bay leaf
2 tablespoons peeled, minced garlic
5 cups Chicken Stock (see recipe on page 184)
1 tablespoon corn starch
2 tablespoons water
1 cup heavy whipping cream
  Salt to taste
  White pepper to taste
¼ cup chopped leaf basil
¼ cup minced chives
1 tablespoon chopped fresh thyme leaf
1 tablespoon chopped fresh oregano
1 tablespoon finely chopped fresh dill
½ pound spinach, stemmed and washed, coarsely chopped
½ cup grated Wisconsin Asiago cheese

Use the surfeit of fresh herbs from your summer garden and create this lovely broth-based soup that is aromatic and delicious.

Melt butter in a heavy bottomed large soup pot. Sauté the onions, over medium heat, until translucent. Do not over cook. Add the bay leaf and garlic; cook 2 minutes. Add the chicken stock; bring to a simmer. Simmer 20 minutes.

In a small bowl mix together corn starch and water. Whisk mixture into soup stock—this will thicken it slightly. Remove bay leaf.

Pour soup mixture into blender and blend until smooth; strain, through a sieve. Return soup mixture to soup pot. Add the cream. Season to taste with salt and pepper. Stir in basil, chives, thyme, oregano, and dill. Stir in spinach and heat until hot throughout. Garnish with grated Asiago cheese and serve.

Ham and Swiss Chowder

yield 12-14 servings

8 cups Chicken Stock (see recipe
on page 184)
4 cups (about 4 medium size)
peeled, cubed potatoes
3 cups chopped onion
3 cups chopped celery
1 tablespoon chopped garlic
1 tablespoon Worcestershire
sauce
1 teaspoon ground black pepper
1 teaspoon ground celery seed
1 teaspoon ground thyme
1 bay leaf
6 cups heavy whipping cream
5 cups diced ham
6 cups grated Wisconsin Baby
Swiss cheese
½ cup butter
½ cup flour

Ham and cheese makes a graceful transition from sandwiches to soup in this recipe. Remember this chowder when winter winds whistle and you want to wrap some warm comfort around family and friends.

In a large kettle bring chicken stock to a boil. Add potatoes, onion, celery, garlic, Worcestershire sauce, black pepper, celery seed, thyme, and bay leaf. Let simmer until potatoes are done. Add cream and heat to just below boiling point. Add ham and then slowly add Swiss cheese, stirring constantly. Set aside.

In a small saucepan, melt butter. Whisk in flour to make a roux and mix until smooth. Add roux to chowder and bring to a boil, stirring as it thickens. Remove bay leaf. Serve.

Corn Sausage Chowder

yield 6 servings

1 pound bulk pork sausage
1 cup coarsely chopped onion
4 cups peeled potatoes, ½-inch dice
1 teaspoon salt
½ teaspoon crushed dried leaf marjoram
⅛ teaspoon freshly ground pepper
2 cups water
1 can cream-style corn (17 ounces)
1 can whole kernel corn (17 ounces), drained
1 can evaporated milk (12 ounces)

We'd like to imagine that our native American Indians originated something similar to this soup. If you like this marriage of flavorful pork sausage, potatoes and corn, consider serving this for a Thanksgiving weekend supper. You might start a new tradition.

In a Dutch oven or kettle, cook sausage and onion until sausage is brown and onion is tender; drain on paper towel.

Return sausage and onion to Dutch oven. Add potatoes, salt, marjoram, pepper, and water. Bring to a boil; reduce heat and simmer just until potatoes are tender, about 15 minutes.

Add cream-style corn, whole kernel corn and evaporated milk. Heat thoroughly and serve.

Salads & Salad Dressings

Salad of the Earth
with Goat Cheese Dressing
4 servings

Salad:
- 1 head red leaf lettuce
- 1 head green oak lettuce
- 1 head Belgian endive
- 4 leaves arugula
- 4 medium size tomatoes
- ½ cup peeled, julienne cucumber
- ½ cup peeled, julienne red onion
- 8 fresh chives for garnish
- ⅓ cup grated Wisconsin Parmesan cheese

Dressing:
- 1 clove garlic, peeled, chopped
  Ground black pepper to taste
- 1 tablespoon chopped fresh basil
- 1 tablespoon chopped fresh parsley
- ½ cup olive oil
- 1½ cups half-and-half
- ¼ cup crumbled Wisconsin goat cheese
- 1 teaspoon balsamic vinegar
  Salt to taste

This signature salad at Cucina is arranged to resemble a beautiful bouquet of edible flowers. Follow our chef's presentation notes to recreate this stunning salad that will have your dinner guests in awe.

To make salad, gently separate all lettuce, endive and arugula leaves and wash in cold water; drain in colander.

Blanch the tomatoes by scalding them quickly in boiling water (about 1 minute). Plunge into ice water; slip off and discard skins. Remove the top of the tomato with a knife and scoop out the seeds. Trim the bottoms off the tomatoes if they do not sit flat on the plate.

Divide the greens; place them stem section first in tomato cups so that they stand up. Set aside.

To make dressing, place garlic, black pepper, basil, parsley, olive oil, and half-and-half in blender. Blend until ingredients are well-mixed. Add goat cheese and vinegar. Blend slightly. Season with salt.

Spoon ¼ cup of goat cheese dressing in the center of a serving plate and arrange the julienne cucumber and red onion. Place the tomato cup in the center and garnish with the chives. Sprinkle with Parmesan cheese and serve.

Photo on page 65

Tomato, Feta and Basil Salad

yield 4 servings

6 roma tomatoes
½ pint yellow cherry tomatoes
1 tablespoon peeled, finely
  chopped shallots
1 tablespoon peeled, finely
  chopped fresh garlic
2 tablespoons finely sliced
  scallions
  Salt to taste
  Black pepper to taste
¼ cup olive oil
1 tablespoon rice wine vinegar
½ cup crumbled feta cheese
2 tablespoons peeled, diced
  Bermuda onion
1 loaf garlic bread, sliced in
  1- 1½ inch slices, warmed in
  oven
2 tablespoons chopped fresh
  basil
2 tablespoons chopped chives
  Cracked black pepper
2 tablespoons grated Wisconsin
  Parmesan cheese

Use fresh-from-the-garden tomatoes, still warm from the sun, for this tasty summer salad that pairs fresh herbs, feta cheese and garlic bread slices together. This is perfect with any grilled main dish entree.

Wash tomatoes. Cut roma tomatoes in eighths; cut cherry tomatoes in half. Place in large bowl; set aside.

In a separate medium bowl mix together shallots, garlic, scallions, salt, pepper, olive oil, vinegar, feta cheese, and onion. Pour mixture over the tomatoes and toss gently.

In the center of an individual serving plate, place one-fourth of the salad. Arrange three slices of bread around salad. Top with fresh basil, chives, cracked black pepper and grated Parmesan cheese.

Tuna Nicoise Salad Sandwich
with Olive Relish
yield 4 servings

Relish:
- 3 tablespoons olive oil
- ½ cup pitted black olives
- ½ cup pitted green olives
- 1 teaspoon peeled, chopped garlic

Salad:
- 9¼ ounces (1½ cans) water-packed tuna, drained
- 2 tablespoons finely diced Bermuda onion
- 2 tablespoons capers, drained
- ¼ cup mayonnaise
- 8 slices hard crust bread
- 8 tomatoes
- 1 cucumber
- 8 leaves fresh spinach

You will never serve an ordinary tuna salad sandwich again after tasting this Mediterranean-inspired sandwich that takes its seasoning secrets from the classic Salad Nicoise. Remember this sandwich when you need to feed a crowd.

To make relish, combine olive oil, black and green olives and garlic in food processor. Process until it is a fine relish. Set aside.

To make salad, in a medium bowl combine tuna, onion, capers and mayonnaise. Mix to blend, do not overmix.

Cut tomatoes and peeled cucumber in ⅛-inch slices. Wash spinach leaves and pat dry.

Spoon and spread olive relish equally on four slices of bread; place tomatoes on top. Spread a ¼-inch layer of tuna salad on the tomatoes and top with cucumber. Place leaf spinach on cucumbers and top with remaining bread slices.

*Chef's Note: You may use any of your favorite breads, mini-French bread or hard rolls.

Grilled Chicken and Roasted Red Pepper Salad

yield 4-6 servings

½ cup vegetable oil
⅛ cup olive oil
1 tablespoon stemmed, chopped fresh thyme
1 teaspoon chopped fresh garlic
1 tablespoon chopped fresh basil
½ teaspoon cracked black peppercorn
½ teaspoon kosher salt
1 pound (approximately) skinless, boneless chicken breasts
1 medium red bell pepper
2 tablespoons finely sliced scallions
½ cup mayonnaise
2 tablespoons rice wine vinegar
Salt to taste
Black pepper to taste

On hot summer nights when the cook is thinking cool thoughts and minimum fuss, this is the pretty salad to prepare. Roasted red bell peppers are simply smashing with herb-infused grilled chicken. (This converts into an excellent sandwich when served with leaf spinach and fresh sprouts on hard-crusted bread.)

Preheat an outdoor grill or grill pan.

In a medium stainless steel bowl combine vegetable oil, olive oil, thyme, garlic, basil, cracked peppercorn and kosher salt.

Coat chicken breasts in herb oil mixture and grill on hot grill until fully cooked, but not dry. (About 5 minutes per side.) Allow to cool to room temperature and dice into ¼-inch cubes.

Place whole red pepper on hot grill until blackened well on the outside. Remove from grill, place in plastic bag and seal. Set aside for 10 minutes. Remove pepper from bag and peel off skin. Slice and remove seeds and dice into ¼-inch cubes.

Blend together chicken, red pepper, scallions, mayonnaise, and rice wine vinegar. Season with salt and pepper to taste and serve chilled.

Fruit & Nut Salad with Yogurt

yield 8-10 servings

½ orange
1 cup vanilla yogurt
1½ teaspoons sugar
1½ pounds green grapes
3 medium green apples
3 medium red apples
½ cup chopped walnuts

Here's a light luncheon salad, easy supper or possibly an after-school-snack for children that is healthy and appealing in every way. The yogurt adds protein to a crunchy, colorful favorite.

Grate zest (outer orange rind) from orange. Squeeze juice from orange. (You should get about ½ teaspoon zest; ¼ cup juice.)

In a large bowl combine yogurt, orange juice, orange zest and sugar. Wash and halve grapes. Cut apples into ½-inch pieces. Combine fruit with yogurt mixture. Fold in walnuts. Stir gently until ingredients are well blended.

Chill and serve.

Chinese Shrimp & Pea Salad

yield 4-6 servings

1 pound frozen peas, thawed
½ pound frozen small salad shrimp, thawed, squeezed dry
2 leeks
6 tablespoons vegetable oil
½ teaspoon Oriental-style sesame oil
½ teaspoon minced garlic
1 cup water chestnuts, drained
¼ teaspoon grated crystallized ginger
½ teaspoon salt
Black pepper to taste
1 tablespoon soy sauce
1 tablespoon rice wine vinegar

Pretty pink shrimp and bright green garden peas have been combined in a plethora of ho-hum ways. Our chefs have breathed new life into this static duo with toasted Oriental-style sesame oil, water chestnuts, crystallized ginger and rice wine vinegar. We think you'll like this Pacific Rim version.

In a large bowl combine peas with the shrimp. Set aside.

Wash leeks thoroughly to remove sand. Trim the top and bottom of leeks, leaving only a small amount of the green top. Slice fine and add to peas and shrimp. Set aside.

In a small bowl combine vegetable oil, sesame oil, garlic, water chestnuts, ginger, salt, pepper, soy sauce, and vinegar. Blend together. Add to peas, shrimp and leeks. Chill.*

*Chef's Note: Salad should be made 24 hours ahead for flavors to blend.

Leaf Spinach & Bibb Lettuce Salad
with Basil Orange Dressing
yield 6 servings

Dressing:

- 4 tablespoons chopped fresh basil
- 2 tablespoons coarsely chopped shallots
- ½ cup Herb Oil (see Freshwater Crayfish Ravioli recipe page 111 for Herb Oil)
- 3 tablespoons orange juice concentrate
- 3 sprigs stemmed, coarsely chopped fresh thyme
- ¼ cup sweet rice wine vinegar
- 1 teaspoon salt
  Pinch black pepper
- 1 tablespoon lemon juice
- 4 ounces sparkling mineral water*

Salad:

- 1 pound fresh leaf spinach
- 1 head bibb lettuce
- ½ cup peeled, julienne red onion
- 6 ounces Wisconsin Asiago cheese, grated or crumbled
- 2 oranges, peeled, separated into segments

Cooks constantly look for ways to reduce fat in their dishes. Here's a lovely salad that begins with flavored herb oil and uses sparkling mineral water to cut back fat calories while still delivering a sweet, tangy taste.

To make dressing, in blender combine fresh basil, shallots, herb oil, orange juice concentrate, fresh thyme, vinegar, salt, pepper, and lemon juice. Set aside.

Wash and stem leaf spinach and bibb lettuce.

To assemble, combine leaf spinach and bibb lettuce in a large bowl; add mineral water to reserved orange dressing and toss with greens. Let stand 10 minutes.

Arrange the onion around the edge of the serving plate and place the greens in the center. Place orange segments on salad. Sprinkle cheese over the salad and serve.

*Chef's Note: The sparkling mineral water will add tang to the dressing.

Photo on page 66

Grilled Vegetable & Pasta Salad

yield 6 servings

Herb Oil Dressing:
- 3 tablespoons vegetable oil
- 1½ teaspoons finely chopped fresh garlic
- 1½ teaspoons chopped fresh thyme
- 1½ teaspoons chopped fresh rosemary
- 1½ teaspoons chopped fresh basil
- 1½ teaspoons cracked black pepper

Salad:
- 1 medium zucchini
- 1 medium yellow squash
- 1 medium red onion
- 4 tomatoes
- 2 green bell peppers
- 2 red bell peppers
- 1 pound dry penne pasta
- 2 tablespoons rice wine vinegar
- Salt to taste
- Black pepper to taste
- Fresh greens of your choice, for garnish
- ¼ cup grated Parmesan cheese

When it is grilling season in your home, consider this fresh, flavorful vegetarian pasta salad. An herb oil marinade flavors the vegetables and pairs well with their lightly smoked character. This salad is tasty served either hot or cold.

To make dressing, in a small bowl whisk together vegetable oil, garlic, thyme, rosemary, basil, and black pepper. Set aside.

Cut zucchini and yellow squash on bias in ¼-inch pieces. Slice red onion in ¼-inch pieces; quarter tomatoes. Cut peppers in pieces about 3 inches square.

Prepare pasta according to package directions. Drain and chill.

Pour reserved herb oil into large bowl. Add zucchini, yellow squash, red onion, tomato, green and red pepper. Toss vegetables in herb oil to coat lightly. Remove vegetables; set aside bowl with remaining herb oil dressing for later use.

Place vegetables in a hot grill pan or on an outdoor grill. Grill 2-3 minutes on each side or until grill marks appear. Remove from grill and lay on ungreased cookie sheet. Cool.

Julienne zucchini, yellow squash, red onion, green and red peppers.

In bowl with remaining herb oil dressing, add vinegar, salt and pepper. Mix well. Add pasta, zucchini, yellow squash, red onion, green and red peppers, and tomatoes. Toss well. Avoid over mixing.

Serve pasta salad on a bed of fresh greens and sprinkle with Parmesan cheese.

This salad can be prepared in advance.

Marinated Spinach, Belgian Endive & Red Leaf Salad
with Sliced Yellow Tomatoes & Cucumbers, Wisconsin Feta Herb Vinaigrette

yield 4 servings

Salad:
- 1 pound leaf spinach
- 2 heads baby red leaf lettuce
- 2 heads Belgian endive
- 4 yellow salad tomatoes (red may be used)
- 2 cucumbers, peeled

Dressing:
- ½ cup vegetable oil
- ⅛ cup rice wine vinegar
- 1 tablespoon peeled, finely chopped shallots
- 1 teaspoon peeled, finely chopped garlic
- 1 tablespoon minced chives
- 1 teaspoon stemmed, finely chopped fresh thyme
- 1 tablespoon stemmed, finely chopped fresh basil
- ⅛ teaspoon ground black pepper
- ¼ cup Wisconsin feta cheese, crumbled

Hot summer days call for cool, light, appealing entrees. Vary the customary salad greens by using these multi-colored, variety lettuces. Feta cheese provides the perfect piquant flavor to this memorable dressing.

Wash all salad ingredients. Stem leaf spinach; remove root ends from red lettuce and endive. Slice tomatoes and cucumbers ⅛-inch thick.

Layer shingle-like, tomatoes and cucumbers in a U-shape on individual serving plates. Lay the Belgian endive spears, 3 per salad coming out of the open spot of the U formed by the tomatoes and cucumbers. Arrange the spinach and lettuce leaves on the endive and sliced tomatoes, allowing endive and tomatoes to show.

For the dressing combine vegetable oil, vinegar, shallots, garlic, chives, thyme, basil, and pepper in a medium bowl and mix well. Spoon dressing over the salad at the time of service and sprinkle with cheese.

Bibb, Radicchio & Watercress Salad
with Wisconsin Asiago & Pistachio Nut Dressing
yield 4 servings

Salad:
- 1 head bibb lettuce
- 1 head radicchio
- 1 bunch watercress, stemmed
- 4 red salad tomatoes

Dressing:
- ½ cup vegetable oil
- ⅛ cup rice wine vinegar
- 1 tablespoon peeled, finely chopped shallots
- 1 teaspoon peeled, minced garlic
- 1 tablespoon minced chives
- ½ teaspoon sugar
- 1 teaspoon finely chopped fresh thyme
- ¼ cup sparkling mineral water*
- 2 tablespoons pistachios, shelled, chopped fine
- 2 tablespoons finely grated Wisconsin Asiago cheese

Does the dressing make the salad? Here's a colorful offering that lets cooks test the theory. If you haven't tried wonderful Wisconsin Asiago cheese before, we urge you to make this dressing. The addition of crunchy pistachio nuts is perfect with this cheese.

In cold water, rinse bibb lettuce, radicchio and watercress; pat dry. Set aside. Slice each salad tomato into five even slices and arrange in a ring on the serving plate. Place leaves of radicchio in the center and the lettuce in the center of the radicchio. Place watercress on top of the lettuce.

To make dressing, in a medium bowl blend vegetable oil, vinegar, shallots, garlic, chives, sugar, and thyme together. Mix well.

Add the sparkling mineral water to the dressing just before serving. Spoon the dressing over the salad and sprinkle liberally with the nuts and cheese. Serve immediately.

*Chef's Note: The sparkling mineral water will add tang to the dressing.

Grilled Vegetable Salad
with Orange Vinaigrette
yield 4 servings

Salad:
- 1 medium zucchini
- 1 medium yellow squash
- 6 plum tomatoes
- 2 medium red onions
- 16 asparagus spears
- 8 green onions
- Salt to taste
- Black pepper to taste
- ¼ cup vegetable oil, for coating vegetables

Orange Vinaigrette:
- 2 oranges
- 1 cup vegetable oil
- ½ cup rice wine vinegar
- ¼ cup finely sliced fresh chives
- 3-4 sprigs fresh thyme, stemmed and chopped
- ½ cup stemmed fresh basil, chopped
- Salt to taste
- Black pepper to taste
- ½ cup sparkling mineral water*
- ¼ cup grated fresh Wisconsin Parmesan or Asiago cheese

Everyone needs a new picnic salad when the occasion calls for a potluck meal. This lightly grilled fresh vegetable salad sports bright colors and fresh garden flavors. The orange-infused vinaigrette adds a light, refreshing flavor.

Wash vegetables for salad. Slice zucchini and squash on bias. Quarter the tomatoes; slice red onions. Trim asparagus and green onions. Season all with salt and pepper and rub lightly with oil. Grill vegetables in a grill pan or on hot outdoor grill. Grill 2-3 minutes on each side or until grill marks appear. Do not overcook. Remove from grill and lay on ungreased cookie sheet. Cool.

Grate zest (outer orange rind) from oranges. Squeeze juice from oranges. (You should get 2 teaspoons zest and 1 cup juice.)

In a medium bowl, combine vegetable oil, vinegar, orange zest, juice, chives, thyme, basil, salt and pepper; whisk together. Add the sparkling mineral water to the dressing just before serving.

Arrange the vegetables on a plate and spoon the dressing over the salad. Sprinkle liberally with cheeses and serve.

*Chef's Note: The sparkling mineral water will add tang to the dressing.

Five Vegetable Slaw
yield 6-8 servings

Vegetable Slaw:
- ½ large head cabbage
- ½ medium red onion
- 1 medium cucumber
- 2 stalks celery
- 1 medium red pepper
- 1 medium green pepper
- 1 carrot
- 1½ teaspoons salt

Dressing:
- 1½ lemons, squeezed for juice (½ cup)
- 1½ cups mayonnaise
- 1½ teaspoons salt
- 2 teaspoons black pepper
- ½ cup sugar
- 1 tablespoon celery seed
- 1 teaspoon cayenne pepper
- 2 tablespoons white vinegar

It may not be red, white and blue but it has most of the colors of Fourth of July fireworks and all the right accompanying "oohs" and "aahs". This is also terrific served with a barbecue pork sandwich.

To make slaw, shred cabbage; thinly slice red onion. Cut cucumber, celery, peppers and carrot in julienne sticks. In a large bowl combine vegetables with salt for 20-30 minutes. Do not add water. (Soaking the vegetables in the salt will reduce the liquid in the vegetables so the slaw will not be runny.) Drain; set aside.

To make dressing, in a medium bowl, combine lemon juice, mayonnaise, salt, black pepper, sugar, celery seed, cayenne pepper, and vinegar.

Add dressing to vegetable slaw and toss gently to combine. Store covered in refrigerator overnight.

Place in strainer to remove excess liquid before serving.

American Club
Red Bliss Potato Salad

yield 4-6 servings

3 pounds red salad potatoes
12 slices uncooked applewood smoked bacon
½ cup red onion, peeled, cut ¼-inch dice
½ cup cucumber, peeled, cut ¼-inch dice
½ cup finely sliced scallions
¼ cup red bell peppers, cut ¼-inch dice
¾ cup vegetable oil
2 tablespoons peeled, chopped garlic
½ teaspoon stemmed, chopped fresh thyme
½ teaspoon stemmed, chopped fresh rosemary
¼ cup minced chives
¼ cup rice wine vinegar
2 tablespoons apple cider vinegar
Salt to taste
Cracked black pepper to taste

All-American potato salad is one of those quintessential recipes handed down from one generation to the next. This chef's favorite has a few colorful twists that add pizazz and good taste. You may want to pass this one on to your children and grandchildren.

Wash the potatoes; place in a 1 gallon pot; cover with water. Bring to simmer and cook until they can be easily pierced with a knife. Drain and allow to cool; slice in quarters and place in a large stainless steel bowl.

In a small sauté pan over medium heat, cook bacon until crisp. Drain fat and reserve bacon.

In a large mixing bowl, combine onions, cucumbers, scallions, red peppers, oil, garlic, thyme, rosemary, chives, vinegars, and crumbled bacon. Season to taste with salt and pepper. Mix to blend ingredients. Pour over the potatoes and toss gently. Do not over mix.

Chill and serve.

Strawberry Spinach Salad
with Sweet Sour Dressing
yield 6 servings

Dressing:
- ½ cup packed light brown sugar
- ½ cup granulated sugar
- ½ cup vinegar

Salad:
- 1 pound fresh spinach
- 3 pints strawberries
- 6 large mushrooms
- ½ cup sliced almonds
- Croutons, for garnish

People who claim they don't like spinach will wind up eating their words as well as their spinach after sampling this beautiful green and red salad with a sweet-sour dressing. Remember this salad during strawberry season or for a holiday dinner splurge.

In a saucepan, combine brown sugar, sugar and vinegar. Stir to dissolve sugars; bring to a boil. Remove from heat; cool.

Remove and discard stems from spinach. Wash and drain leaves. Break spinach in bite-size pieces into salad bowl.

Remove stems from strawberries and wash. Slice strawberries over spinach.

Slice mushrooms and arrange on salad. Sprinkle almonds over salad.

Garnish with croutons. Serve dressing on the side.

Spa English Cucumber & Dill Dressing

yield 1 ⅓ cups

Herb Oil:
- 2 tablespoons vegetable oil
- ½ clove garlic, finely chopped
- Pinch of fresh thyme, chopped
- Pinch of fresh rosemary, chopped
- Pinch of fresh basil, chopped
- Cracked black pepper, to taste

Dressing:
- ½ English (seedless) cucumber
- 1½ tablespoons honey mustard
- Dash hot sauce
- Salt to taste
- Black pepper to taste
- 1 tablespoon chopped shallots
- 4 sprigs fresh dill, chopped
- ¼ cup chilled raspberry-flavored sparkling mineral water

Health-conscious guests at the American Club have come to request this dressing that replaces some of the oil with sparkling mineral water. Wonderful flavors and textures combined with reduced fat make this a winning creation.

In a small bowl, blend together with a whisk, vegetable oil, garlic, thyme, rosemary, basil, and black pepper. Set aside.

To make dressing, peel cucumber and cut in 1-inch chunks. In blender, combine cucumber, honey mustard, hot sauce, salt and pepper, reserved herb oil, and shallots. Blend until smooth.

Pour into a small bowl and stir in dill. Add chilled raspberry-flavored sparkling mineral water just before serving. Store, covered, in refrigerator.

Parmesan Dressing

yield 2 cups

⅔ cup mayonnaise
⅔ cup buttermilk
½ cup sour cream
¼ cup grated Parmesan
   cheese
⅛ cup finely diced onion
1½ teaspoons Worcestershire
   sauce
3 dashes hot sauce
1 teaspoon salt
¼ teaspoon pepper
   Pinch dry mustard
1 teaspoon garlic powder
1 teaspoon lemon juice

Some folks like a dressing that clings to their salad greens—one that they don't have to chase all over their salad plates. This thick-and-creamy dressing is bound to please those salad dressing purists.

In a medium bowl, combine mayonnaise, buttermilk, sour cream, Parmesan cheese, and onion. With a large spoon or a whisk, mix until blended.

Add Worcestershire sauce, hot sauce, salt, pepper, dry mustard, garlic, and lemon juice. Mix until well blended.

Store, covered, in refrigerator.

Smokey French Dressing

yield 2¾ cups

¾ cup sugar
⅓ cup white vinegar
½ cup catsup
⅛ cup diced onion
  Salt to taste
  Cracked black pepper,
  to taste
1½ cups vegetable oil
1½ teaspoons Worcestershire
  sauce
 1 teaspoon liquid smoke

You will love this simple-to-make, smokey flavored classic from the American Club kitchens.

Combine sugar, white vinegar, catsup, onion, salt, cracked black pepper, oil, Worcestershire, and liquid smoke in a blender. Mix until smooth and blended.

Store, covered, in refrigerator.

Lime Honey Mustard Dressing

yield 2½ cups

⅓ cup honey mustard
2 large egg yolks*
1½ cups vegetable oil
⅓ cup rice wine vinegar
1 lime
Salt to taste
Freshly ground black
pepper to taste
2 cloves garlic, peeled,
chopped
1 tablespoon shallots, peeled,
chopped

There is something quite irresistible about the combination of fresh lime and honey in a dressing. It teases you with its pleasant tartness and satisfies you with its hint of sweetness.

Combine the honey mustard and egg yolks in a blender; add the vegetable oil and rice wine vinegar.

Grate lime zest (green outer rind); set aside. Squeeze juice from lime. (You should get about 1 teaspoon zest and ¼ cup juice.) Add the lime juice, zest, salt, pepper, garlic, and shallots; blend until smooth.

Store, covered, in refrigerator.

*Chef's Note: If raw eggs are a concern to you, you may use an egg substitute.

Hot Maple Walnut Dressing

yield 1½ quarts

¼ cup chopped fresh ginger root
1 teaspoon powdered mustard
½ teaspoon celery seed
2 tablespoons packed brown sugar
½ cup chopped walnuts
½ teaspoon paprika
½ teaspoon salt
½ cup diced onion
1 tablespoon butter or margarine
1 pint mayonnaise
2 tablespoons white wine
1 tablespoon lemon juice
1 cup sour cream
2 tablespoons maple sugar

This "House Dressing" at Blackwolf Run can be made ahead and stored in the refrigerator. When you want to transform ordinary greens into something special, simply heat up this flavorful dressing and serve it warm.

In a small bowl mix ginger root, mustard, celery seed, brown sugar, walnuts, paprika, and salt.

Using a medium-sized saucepan, sauté the diced onion in the butter or margarine over medium heat. Reduce heat to low. Combine mayonnaise, white wine, lemon juice, sour cream, and sugar with sautéed onion. Add the spice mixture to the sautéed ingredients. Heat on low; do not boil (it will separate if you let it boil). Serve hot.

Refrigerate unused dressing. Dressing may be heated in small amounts in a microwave oven.

Garlic Marsala Dressing

yield 6 cups

1½ tablespoons chopped garlic
¼ cup stemmed parsley, washed
1¼ cups olive oil
1¼ cups vegetable oil
1 tablespoon sugar
1⅛ cups balsamic vinegar
2 tablespoons stemmed, chopped fresh thyme
2 tablespoons stemmed, chopped fresh basil
1 cup Marsala wine
2 tablespoons grated Wisconsin Parmesan cheese

The next time you plan an Italian entree and serve a large crisp green salad, pull out this dressing recipe for the perfect flavor pairing. Balsamic vinegar and Marsala wine coupled with fresh herbs and cheese make this the right stuff.

Put garlic, parsley, olive oil, vegetable oil, sugar, vinegar, thyme, basil, Marsala, and Parmesan cheese in a blender. Blend until smooth.

Shake or whip before using.

Seared Walleye
with Papaya Relish and
Mango Butter Sauce

Recipe on page 5

**Great Lakes Smoked
Chub Chowder**

Recipe on page 31

Fire & Ice Soup

Hot Grilled Shrimp with Chilled Gazpacho and Avocado Relish

Recipe on page 35

Salad of the Earth
with Goat Cheese Dressing

Recipe on page 43

**Leaf Spinach &
Bibb Lettuce Salad**
with Basil Orange Dressing

Recipe on page 49

**Seared
Veal Tenderloin**
*Salad of Spinach and Basil
Sliced Pears and Fresh
Wisconsin Parmesan*

Recipe on page 134

Clockwise from left:

**Smoked Cheddar
Cheese Brioche,
Whole Wheat
Walnut Bread,
Finnish Cardamom
Bread,
Swedish Limpa
Rye Bread**

Recipes on
pages 22, 20, 17, 16

Grilled Primavera Pizza   Recipe on page 75

Pizza Dough   *at right*   Recipe on page 23

Tiramisu   *in upper left corner*   Recipe on page 158

Wood-Fired Loin of Venison
Barbecue Vinaigrette, Grilled Potato Salad,
Marinated Cucumber, Red Onion and Tomatoes

Recipe on page 123

Seared Fillet of Fresh Walleye
with Toasted Sesame Crust

Recipe on page 110

**Fillet of
Norwegian Salmon**
*Tomato, Cucumber Salad
and Potato Crisps*

Recipe on page 106

**Pan Grilled
Medallions of Pork**
*Warm Salad of French
Beans, Cucumbers and
Orange Segments,
Poupon Mustard Spa
Basil Vinaigrette*

Recipe on page 129

Pizza, Pasta & Side Dishes

Cucina's Traditional Pizza

yield one 10-inch pizza

¼ cup sundried tomatoes, sliced ¼-inch pieces

½ cup water

1 Pizza Dough recipe (see recipe on page 23)

½ cup Roasted Tomato Garlic Pizza Sauce (see recipe on page 176)

1 cup Italian sausage, roasted, sliced ¼-inch thick

⅛ cup roasted garlic cloves, peeled

1 cup grated Wisconsin mozzarella cheese

½ cup grated Wisconsin Parmesan cheese

2 tablespoons chopped fresh basil

This signature pizza from Cucina Restaurant features homemade dough, roasted garlic cloves and tomato pizza sauce, Italian sausage, a mixture of Wisconsin cheeses, and of course, fresh basil. Traditional flavors triumph in this classic pizza.

In a medium bowl, place tomatoes in water to hydrate them. Let stand for approximately 30 minutes. Drain before use.

Roll pizza dough into a 10-inch round. Place on pizza screen. Bake in preheated 400-degree oven for 4 minutes.

Spread pizza sauce on crust within one inch of the edge. Arrange sausage and garlic on pizza; sprinkle cheeses evenly on the top. Scatter tomatoes and basil over cheese.

Bake in a preheated 400-degree oven 10-12 minutes or until cheese is melted and crust is crisp.

Cut and serve hot.

Four Cheese and Spinach Pizza

yield one 10-inch pizza

1 Pizza Dough recipe (see recipe on page 23)
2 tablespoons Basil Pesto (see recipe on page 171)
1½ pounds fresh spinach, washed, stemmed, chopped lightly
½ cup grated Wisconsin smoked provolone cheese
½ cup grated Wisconsin mozzarella cheese
½ cup crumbled Wisconsin feta cheese
¼ cup grated Wisconsin Romano cheese
½ cup pitted sliced black olives
½ cup onions, sliced in ¼-inch thick rings

Combine four cheeses made in Wisconsin—smoked provolone, mozzarella, feta and Romano and you get flavor in abundance. Add some basil pesto, fresh spinach and black olives and you have created a taste sensation.

Roll pizza dough into a 10-inch round. Place on pizza screen. Bake in preheated 400-degree oven for 4 minutes.

Brush basil pesto evenly over the pizza dough. Top with spinach. Sprinkle grated cheeses evenly over spinach. Top with olives and onions.

Bake in a preheated 400-degree oven 8-10 minutes or until cheese is melted and crust is crisp.

Cut and serve hot.

Grilled Primavera Pizza

yield one 10-inch pizza

½ cup red onions, cut in ¼-inch slices

½ cup green bell pepper, julienne cut

½ cup zucchini, sliced ¼-inch thick

½ cup button mushrooms, sliced ¼-inch thick

½ cup vegetable oil

2 teaspoons peeled, finely chopped fresh garlic

1 tablespoon finely chopped fresh basil leaves

½ teaspoon stemmed, finely chopped fresh rosemary

½ teaspoon salt

½ teaspoon black pepper

1 Pizza Dough recipe (see recipe on page 23)

½ cup Roasted Tomato Garlic Pizza Sauce (see recipe on page 176)

1 cup grated Wisconsin aged mozzarella cheese

½ cup grated Wisconsin Asiago cheese

1 tablespoon minced chives

One way to get your family and friends to eat their vegetables (and enjoy them) is to grill the vegetables to tender crispness and then use the medley as a vegetarian pizza filling.

Preheat an outdoor grill to high heat.

In a large mixing bowl, toss onions, peppers, zucchini and mushrooms with oil, garlic, basil, rosemary, salt and pepper.

Grill vegetables on hot grill until partially cooked. Reserve.

Roll pizza dough into a 10-inch round. Place on pizza screen. Bake in preheated 400-degree oven for 4 minutes.

Spread pizza sauce on crust within one inch of the edge. Arrange vegetables evenly on crust. Sprinkle the cheeses over vegetables.

Bake in a preheated 400-degree oven 10-12 minutes or until cheese is melted and crust is crisp.

Sprinkle with chives; cut and serve hot.

Photo on page 67

Pasta Dough

yield 4 servings

½ cup semolina flour
1½ cups all-purpose flour
4 large eggs
Extra all-purpose flour for
kneading
Extra semolina flour for
dusting

If you love fresh pasta, you will want to try this made-from-scratch dough in your home kitchen. You will need a pasta machine (manual is fine) and a partner to share in the fun. This dough works well in nearly every pasta recipe.

Sift both flours onto flat surface and make a well in the center. Beat 4 eggs and pour into well. With fingertips, mix together until the dough is soft and begins to stick together. When the dough comes together, knead dough with heal of hand for 10-15 minutes. Set aside and let rest for 1 hour.

Roll out dough and place in pasta machine on lowest numerical setting, working the dough thinner each time until it is approximately ¹⁄₁₆-inch thick. Dust pasta dough with semolina flour to prevent sticking.

Cut in desired shapes and proceed with recipe of your choice.

Pasta With Gorgonzola Sauce

yield 4 cups

1½ teaspoons chopped shallots
1½ teaspoons chopped garlic
1 teaspoon chopped fresh basil
1 tablespoon butter
1 cup Chicken Stock (see recipe on page 184)
3 cups heavy whipping cream
¼ pound Gorgonzola cheese or blue cheese
2 tablespoons cornstarch
2 tablespoons cold water
Dash cayenne pepper
Salt to taste
White pepper to taste
1 pound cooked orzo pasta or pasta of your choice

Gorgonzola cheese is milder than other blue-veined cheeses and very smooth and special on the palate. If you like blue cheeses, but don't want to overwhelm family and friends with too-sharp flavors, this is a lovely recipe to make.

In a 12-inch skillet, sauté shallots, garlic and basil in butter. Add chicken stock; simmer 10 minutes. Add heavy cream and cheese stirring constantly. Combine cornstarch and water; whisk into sauce to thicken. Season to taste with cayenne pepper, salt and pepper. Combine with cooked pasta.

Wisconsin Parmesan Polenta
with Gorgonzola Cream and Grilled Vegetables
yield 6 servings

Polenta:
- 7½ cups water
- Salt to taste
- 1 finely chopped clove garlic
- 2⅔ cups cornmeal (white or stone ground)
- ⅓ cup grated fresh Wisconsin Parmesan cheese
- ¼ cup grated fresh Wisconsin Asiago cheese
- Olive oil

Grilled Vegetables:
- 3 medium zucchini, cut in strips
- 1 large Bermuda or red onion, cut in rings
- 1 medium red bell pepper, cut in strips
- 9 cherry tomatoes, halved
- 12 small button mushrooms
- 12 small oyster mushrooms
- Olive oil
- Salt to taste
- Black pepper to taste
- Rice wine vinegar to taste

Sauce:
- Olive oil
- 1 tablespoon chopped fresh garlic
- 3 tablespoons chopped fresh shallots
- 2 quarts heavy whipping cream
- 8 ounces Gorgonzola cheese
- 2 tablespoons chopped fresh basil
- 2 teaspoons chopped chives
- 1 teaspoon chopped fresh thyme
- 1 teaspoon prepared mustard
- Parmesan cheese, for garnish

Crisp, golden brown crusted polenta, that Italian staple, is served with Pepper Crusted Veal Tenderloin (recipe page 133) for an outstanding entree. Two Wisconsin cheeses flavor this cornmeal-based side dish that is beautiful served with accompanying grilled vegetables.

Bring the water to boil in a large heavy pot. Season with salt; add garlic. Stir in the cornmeal until thoroughly mixed and smooth. With a wooden spoon, stir the polenta over medium heat until it comes away from the sides of the pot, about 10 minutes. Remove from heat and stir in cheeses. Pour out onto a greased 11x15-inch jelly roll pan and chill until firm.

Place vegetables on cookie sheet. Coat lightly with olive oil and season with salt and pepper. Shake off excess oil before grilling. In hot dry grill pan, grill the vegetables making crisscross marks. Toss the grilled vegetables lightly with rice wine vinegar and reserve.

To make sauce, heat olive oil in a medium sauce pot and sauté the garlic and shallots; add cream; bring to boil. Stir in the cheese and simmer for five minutes. Add basil, chives, thyme and mustard. Reserve.

Remove polenta from refrigerator. Cut into diamond shapes. Put a small amount of olive oil in a sauté pan and sauté the polenta until golden brown. Place on plate in the shape of the Mercedes symbol. Fold the zucchini strips in half and alternate between the polenta. Arrange the grilled vegetables in the center of the plate. Spoon the polenta with sauce; dust with fresh grated Wisconsin Parmesan.

Mushroom and Scallion Wild Rice Blend

yield 4-6 servings

4½ cups Chicken Stock (divided)
　　(see recipe on page 184)
　　Salt to taste
　　Black pepper to taste
½ cup uncooked brown rice
½ cup uncooked wild rice
2 tablespoons butter (divided)
½ cup finely diced Spanish onion
½ cup uncooked white rice
1 bay leaf
1 teaspoon chopped garlic
1 cup sliced button mushrooms
½ cup finely sliced scallions

The marriage of three types of rice (wild, brown and white), give this special occasion side dish its nut-like flavor and texture. We like to serve this with our Pan Grilled Medallions of Veal Loin (recipe on page 132).

Season chicken stock with salt and pepper. In a separate small saucepan put 1½ cups of chicken stock and add brown rice. Bring to a boil, reduce to simmer; cover and cook until tender, about 50 minutes. Reserve.

In a small heavy bottomed saucepan, put 1½ cups of chicken stock and add wild rice. Bring to a boil, reduce to simmer; cover and cook until tender, but not split apart, about 35 minutes. Reserve.

In a medium sauté pan, melt 1 tablespoon of butter and add diced onion. Sauté over medium heat until the onions are translucent. Add white rice and stir to coat. Add the remaining 1½ cups chicken stock and bay leaf. Simmer until rice is tender.

Combine all three types of rice and reserve.*

In a medium sauté pan, melt the remaining 1 tablespoon butter and sauté chopped garlic, mushrooms and scallions. Sauté until mushrooms are tender and begin to render out the juices. Combine with rice and serve.

*Chef's Note: The rice may be cooked in advance and held under refrigeration. In order to heat it again, gently warm with some chicken stock, then fold in mushroom-scallion mixture.

Ragu of Smoked Onions

yield 4 servings

½ cup hickory chips
2 medium size red onions
2 tablespoons vegetable oil
2 tablespoons butter
1 tablespoon chopped garlic
1 teaspoon sugar
1 tablespoon rice wine vinegar
   Salt to taste
   Black pepper to taste

If you haven't smoked onions over hickory chips on your grill, you are missing out on a taste sensation. Whether your main dish is upscale like Veal Medallions (recipe on page 132) or homestyle like hamburger, these onions will add something special.

Soak hickory chips in water for 24 hours.

Preheat an outdoor grill to high heat.

Peel and slice onions ¼-inch thick; brush with oil.

Shake the excess water from the hickory chips and toss them on the hot coals. Wait 2-5 minutes until they begin to produce smoke; arrange the onions on the grill. Close the lid and smoke for 20 minutes. (The heat of the grill must be turned down at this time so hickory chips do not flame up.) When the onions are smoked, remove from grill. Set aside.

Melt butter in a sauté pan and add garlic. Lightly sauté; add smoked onions, sugar, vinegar, salt and pepper. Toss until the onions are soft and the juices evaporate; serve.

This can be prepared in advance and reheated when it is needed.

Ratatouille of Grilled Vegetables

yield 4 servings

1 medium size zucchini
1 medium size yellow squash
1 Bermuda onion
1 medium red bell pepper
1 medium green bell pepper
2 plum tomatoes
½ cup vegetable oil
Salt to taste
Black pepper to taste
1 teaspoon stemmed, chopped fresh basil
1 teaspoon peeled, chopped garlic

Ratatouille, that classic Mediterranean vegetable dish, takes on new excitement, textures and flavors with this innovative grilled preparation. We suggest serving this with our Loin of Midwestern Lamb (recipe on page 127).

Preheat outdoor grill or grill pan.

Slice the zucchini and yellow squash lengthwise into ¼-inch thick slices. Peel onion; slice into ¼-inch rings. Quarter peppers and remove seeds; halve tomatoes.

Lightly coat vegetables with oil and season with salt and pepper. Grill vegetables on hot charcoal grill or grill pan. Do not burn or overcook the vegetables.

Remove vegetables; while still warm, dice the vegetables into a ¼-inch dice and season with basil and garlic.

Toss lightly to blend ingredients. This may be chilled and eaten cold as a salad or reheated when needed.

Smoked Onion and Roasted Potato Salad

yield 4 servings

½ cup hickory chips soaked in water 24 hours
½ cup peeled, sliced onion
½ cup vegetable oil
1 pound new potatoes, washed
Salt to taste
Black pepper to taste
¼ teaspoon chopped fresh rosemary (dry cannot be used)
½ teaspoon chopped garlic
⅛ cup rice wine vinegar
1 tablespoon chopped chives

Once you've tasted smoked onions from the grill, no doubt you'll want to add their robust flavor to other dishes. This roasted potato salad is just the right flavor partner. Pair this with Farm-Raised Pheasant Breast (recipe on page 98) or any grilled chicken or turkey dish.

Preheat an outdoor charcoal grill. Place the wet hickory wood chips on the hot charcoal and wait until they begin to smoke. Place onions on grill and close the lid. Smoke for 20 minutes; do not burn the onions. When finished, cool onions and cut into ¼-inch dice.

Coat potatoes well with vegetable oil and season with salt and pepper. Place potatoes on a cookie sheet. Bake in a preheated 350-degree oven until the potatoes are cooked, approximately 20 minutes. (Reserve oil left on cookie sheet). Cut the potatoes in fourths while still warm; toss gently (as not to mash) with the rosemary, garlic, vinegar, smoked onions, and oil left on cookie sheet. Sprinkle with chives and serve warm.

Wild Rice Potato Cakes

yield 4 servings

3 cups peeled, grated russet potatoes
1 cup wild rice, cooked
½ cup finely sliced scallions
¼ cup peeled, coarsely chopped shallots
Salt to taste
Black pepper to taste
2 large eggs, beaten
½ cup vegetable oil or butter (divided)

Undecided whether to serve potatoes or rice as a side dish? Why not serve both together, in these tasty pan-fried cakes that complement Duck Confit (recipe on page 95) or any wild game entree.

In large bowl, combine potatoes, rice, scallions, shallots, and season with salt and pepper. Let stand for 5 minutes. With your hands, take the potato mixture and squeeze out as much water as possible. Add eggs to potato mixture and blend well.

Heat a 10-inch sauté pan to medium heat. Add ¼ cup of oil or butter to pan. Portion the potato mixture into 8 even pancakes. Place 4 pancakes in skillet. Flatten carefully with a spatula and allow to cook to golden brown on both sides, approximately 3-5 minutes. Add additional oil if needed. Remove and keep warm. Add remaining ¼ cup oil or butter to pan. Cook remaining pancakes. Serve warm.

Photo on page 135

Potato Pancakes

yield 4 servings

1¾ pounds potatoes
½ cup peeled, sliced onion
1 large egg, beaten
1 teaspoon salt
¼ teaspoon baking powder
1 tablespoon heavy whipping
   cream
1 teaspoon lemon juice
   Nutmeg to taste (optional)
   Garlic to taste (optional)
   Vegetable oil

On those lovely mornings when brunch is leisurely, take the time to make these comforting potato pancakes. Serve them with a favorite maple or fruit-flavored syrup, homemade jam or apple butter.

Peel potatoes. In a food processor, grind potatoes and onions coarsely. Transfer to colander and press potato mixture against side of colander to remove excess liquid.

In a medium bowl, combine potatoes, onions, egg, salt, baking powder, cream, and lemon juice. Add nutmeg and garlic if desired. Mix thoroughly and shape into 4-inch pancakes.

Fry pancakes in a 12-inch skillet in hot oil, turning once; fry until golden brown. Serve hot.

Potato and Pear Flan

yield 6-8 servings

1 tablespoon butter
8 baker potatoes (approximately 4 pounds)
2 Bartlett pears (approximately 1 pound)
8 ounces grated Wisconsin Asiago cheese
8 ounces grated Wisconsin Parmesan cheese
8 large eggs
1 quart half-and-half
2 teaspoons chopped garlic
  Salt to taste
  Black pepper to taste
  Dash nutmeg

Who, besides the American Club chefs, would think of combining potatoes and pears in a side dish? Trust our talented staff and make this grand side dish that is sublime with our Pine Nut Crusted Rack of Lamb (recipe on page 125).

Butter a 9x13-inch baking pan. Peel potatoes and pears; slice to $\frac{1}{16}$-inch thickness. Layer potatoes, pears and grated cheeses in baking pan. (The flan should only be 1-inch high.)

In a medium bowl, beat eggs and half-and-half; add garlic. Season with salt, pepper and nutmeg. Blend well. Pour the egg mixture over the potato dish until it reaches the level of the potatoes.

Bake in a preheated 300-degree oven for approximately 45-60 minutes or until golden brown. Chill and slice into desired-size wedges. Can serve cold or it may be reheated.

Photo on page 137

Gratin Dauphinois

yield 8 servings

2 pounds baking potatoes
1 tablespoon butter
 Granulated garlic to taste
1 cup grated Wisconsin Gruyère
 cheese or a mixture of Swiss
 and Parmesan cheese
2 cups milk
1⅓ cups heavy whipping cream
2 large eggs
 Salt to taste
 Black pepper to taste
 Nutmeg to taste

This delightful variation from the too-typical au gratin potatoes uses cheese, a bit of garlic and nutmeg for its superb creamy flavors. Remember this recipe when your menu needs a substantial side dish.

Peel and wash potatoes; slice thin, ⅛-inch, like you would for scalloped potatoes. Rinse in warm water to eliminate some of the starch. Pat dry with a towel.

Rub butter and garlic over the inside of a 9x13-inch casserole dish. Put a single layer of potatoes in casserole, then a layer of cheese. Repeat these steps until all potatoes and cheese have been used. Finish with a layer of cheese.

In a medium bowl, mix milk, cream, eggs, salt, pepper, and nutmeg; pour over potatoes. With a spoon or your hand, press down potatoes to distribute liquid; smooth top of potatoes.

Bake, covered, in a preheated 375-degree oven for 35 minutes. Uncover and cook for an additional 10-15 minutes or until golden brown and tender.

Poultry

Macadamia Nut-Crusted Chicken Breast 89
with Buerre Blanc

Rosemary Seared Breast of Chicken 91
Roasted Corn, Leeks and Applewood Smoked Bacon

Smoked Chicken and Angel Hair Pasta 92
Basil Pesto Cream and Pine Nuts

Hickory Smoked Duck Breast and Gulf Shrimp . . 93
with Salad of Seasonal Greens and Yellow Tomato Vinaigrette

Duckling Confit 95
Corn Relish and Wild Rice Potato Cakes

Roast Duck 97
with Door County Cherry Sauce and Cinnamon Toasted Almonds

Farm Raised Pheasant Breast 98
*with Chardonnay Wine, White Grapes and Chanterelles,
Warm Smoked Onions and Roasted Potato Salad*

Oven Roasted Cornish Game Hens 99
Wild Mushrooms, Roasted Shallots and Natural Jus

Macadamia Nut-Crusted Chicken Breast
with Buerre Blanc
yield 8 servings

Seasoned Flour:
- 2 cups flour
- 2 tablespoons salt
- 1 teaspoon black pepper
- 1 teaspoon granulated garlic

Seasoned Bread Crumbs:
- 2 cups dry bread crumbs
- 1 tablespoon salt
- 1 teaspoon black pepper
- 1 tablespoon chopped fresh thyme
- 3 tablespoons chopped macadamia nuts

Salsa:
- ¾ cup fresh pineapple, peeled and diced
- ½ cup diced Bermuda onion
- ½ cup diced green bell pepper
- ½ cup diced red bell pepper

Chicken Breasts:
- 8 chicken breasts (5 ounces each)
- 4 large eggs, beaten
- 1 cup vegetable oil
- 1 orange, for garnish
- 1 small bunch daikon sprouts, for garnish

This is one of those great dishes that carries enough flavors and textures to launch your friends into a guessing frenzy over the ingredient list. Serve this tender chicken entree with fruit salsa and lovely butter sauce and let the guessing begin.

In medium bowl, combine flour, salt, pepper and granulated garlic. Mix well; set aside.

In another medium bowl, combine bread crumbs, salt, pepper, thyme, and nuts. Mix well; set aside.

In a small bowl, mix pineapple, onion and peppers together and let stand. Cover and refrigerate.

Dip chicken breast in seasoned flour, egg and then seasoned breading. Heat vegetable oil in a 12-inch skillet; add chicken, cook over medium heat until lightly browned. Finish in a preheated 325-degree oven, for approximately 10 minutes. Be careful not to over bake.

To prepare Buerre Blanc, sauté shallots and garlic in 1 tablespoon butter in a large saucepan; add white wine, bay leaf, thyme, lemon juice, lime juice, cider vinegar; reduce to almost nothing (be careful not to burn). Add heavy cream and reduce again. Reduce heat to low. Whip remaining butter into sauce in small pieces, allowing each to melt before adding another piece. Add apricot preserves; season with cayenne pepper, salt and pepper. Remove bay leaf.

To serve, slice chicken breasts in half, lay one half in center of plate horizontally, spoon pine-

Buerre Blanc:
- ⅓ **cup chopped shallots**
- ¼ **teaspoon chopped garlic**
- 1 **pound butter, room temperature (divided)**
- 1 **cup chardonnay wine**
- 1 **bay leaf**
- ¼ **teaspoon chopped fresh thyme**
   Juice of 1 lemon (½ cup)
- 1 **tablespoon lime juice**
- 2 **tablespoons cider vinegar**
- 1 **tablespoon heavy whipping cream**
- 2 **tablespoons apricot preserves**
- 2 **dashes cayenne pepper**
   Salt to taste
   Black pepper to taste

apple salsa along side of chicken breast. Lay other half of chicken breast vertically, so that it forms a "T" shape. Peel and slice orange into ¼-inch slices, lay two slices overlapping at three points of a triangle. Drizzle sauce over top of chicken, tuck daikon sprouts under top breast, so that they stand up.

Rosemary Seared Breast of Chicken
Roasted Corn, Leeks and Applewood Smoked Bacon
yield 4 servings

2 tablespoons vegetable oil
1 tablespoon stemmed, chopped fresh rosemary
Salt to taste
Black pepper to taste
4 chicken breasts (7 ounces each), wing bone on, skin on, breast bone removed
½ cup chardonnay
2 cups Brown Chicken Stock (see recipe on page 185)

Corn, Leeks and Bacon:
4 ears of corn, whole with husks, corn silk removed (soak in salted water for 30 minutes)
½ cup diced ¼-inch apple wood smoked bacon, fried crisp, (reserve 1 tablespoon of bacon fat)
½ cup peeled, diced ¼-inch red onions
1 teaspoon finely chopped garlic
½ cup julienne cut red bell pepper
½ cup julienne cut leeks, white and green parts

In late summer, when sweet corn is its very sweetest, try this rustic main dish that combines chicken, corn, wood-smoked bacon, leeks, and red bell pepper in a charming, upscale country dish.

Combine oil, rosemary, salt and pepper. Marinate the chicken in this mixture for 2 hours minimum, or overnight if possible.

Heat a heavy 12-inch sauté pan to medium heat and add the marinated chicken breasts, skin side down. Sear the chicken until it is golden brown. Turn carefully so skin does not tear. Sear second side. Remove chicken from sauté pan and place it in oven proof baking dish. Add chardonnay and place in a preheated 350-degree oven for approximately 35-40 minutes or until the internal temperature is 135 degrees. Add the chicken stock in small quantities to prevent the bottom of the pan from becoming too dark.

Shake excess water from corn and grill on preheated outdoor grill until husk is totally black. Remove from grill and remove husk; with a knife remove kernels from cob. This can be done a day in advance.

In a 12-inch sauté pan over medium heat, add reserved fat, onion, garlic and red pepper, toss until lightly cooked. Add corn and bacon to warm through.

In a separate small sauté pan place leeks with enough water to cover them. Simmer 1-2 minutes to wilt; drain off water.

Spoon corn in the center of the serving plate. Slice the breast of chicken on a bias about a half inch thick and fan out over the corn. Spoon the natural juices over the chicken. Sprinkle with leeks and serve.

Smoked Chicken and Angel Hair Pasta
Basil Pesto Cream and Pine Nuts
yield 4 servings

1 cup hickory chips, soaked in water, for 24 hours

4 boneless, skinless chicken breasts (5 ounces each)
Salt to taste
Black pepper to taste

½ pound angel hair pasta (dry weight)

¼ cup olive oil

¾ cup Basil Pesto (see recipe on page 171)

1½ cups heavy whipping cream

½ cup grated Wisconsin Parmesan cheese

½ cup toasted pine nuts

Cucina Restaurant takes a traditional Italian preparation and transforms it into a tasty signature dish by adding house-smoked chicken. You will like the marriage of basil, Parmesan cheese and pine nuts that is quintessential pesto.

Preheat an outdoor grill to medium high heat. Shake off excess water from hickory chips; place on hot briquettes. Season chicken breasts with salt and pepper and arrange on the grill; close the lid and smoke for 15-20 minutes. If the chips flame, sprinkle them with water to extinguish. Allow the chicken breast to fully cook; slice into strips and reserve.

Cook the angel hair in boiling water until al dente, drain. Toss in olive oil; reserve.

In a large 12-inch sauté pan, combine the pesto and heavy cream, bring to a boil, and add chicken strips. Toss with reserved angel hair pasta.

Divide pasta mixture between four serving plates and sprinkle with Parmesan cheese and pine nuts. Serve hot.

Hickory Smoked Duck Breast and Gulf Shrimp
with Salad of Seasonal Greens and Yellow Tomato Vinaigrette
yield 4 servings

Vinaigrette:
- 1 **cup orange juice**
- 2 **cups vegetable oil**
- ½ **cup rice wine vinegar**
- 1 **lemon**
- 2 **tablespoons chopped fresh parsley**
- 2 **tablespoons chopped fresh chives**
- 1 **tablespoon chopped fresh thyme**
- 3-4 **medium-sized peeled, finely chopped shallots**
- 1 **clove finely chopped garlic**
  Salt to taste
  White pepper to taste
- 1 **pint yellow or red cherry tomatoes, cut in half**

Duck:
- 1 **cup hickory chips, soaked in water for 24 hours**
- 4 **duck breasts (6-8 ounces each) skin on**
- 16 **shrimp (10-15 count) peeled, deveined**

Salad:
- 12 **leaves radicchio**
- 12 **leaves spinach**
- 12 **leaves red oak lettuce**
- 12 **leaves bibb lettuce**
- ½ **cup julienne cut shiitake mushrooms**
- ½ **cup julienne cut leeks**
- ½ **cup julienne cut tomatoes, seeded**

Duck breasts are fun to cook with. They are simple to do and slice beautifully in a salad presentation. This dish that incorporates hickory-smoked duck breasts was served on a hot summer day at Cucina. It bears repeating.

In a large bowl, whisk together orange juice, oil, vinegar, juice of lemon, parsley, chives, thyme, shallots, garlic, salt and pepper. Add tomatoes and gently toss. Refrigerate covered for 24 hours. Stir before use.

Preheat outdoor grill, and place the soaked hickory chips on the hot briquettes. Wait until they begin to smoke and turn the heat down, to prevent them from catching fire.

Place the duck breasts on the grill and close the lid. Smoke for 20 minutes. If the hickory chips begin to catch fire, wet them with water from a squirt bottle.

Remove the duck breasts and place the shrimp on the grill, smoke for 5 minutes and remove. This can be done in advance if needed.

Preheat a heavy bottomed 12-inch sauté pan and place the duck breast skin side down; sear over medium heat for 15 minutes, or cook until they are medium. Pour off fat that will render from the skin and reserve. Reserve the duck breast in a warm place. Sauté the shrimp to ensure they are fully cooked, using reserved duck fat if needed. Remove and reserve in a warm place.

Wash radicchio, spinach and lettuce; pat dry and set aside.

Lightly sauté shiitake mushrooms and leeks in sauté pan.

To serve, arrange the greens in the center of four serving plates. Place the leeks, mushrooms and tomatoes around the spinach, and lay the shrimp on them evenly.

Slice each duck breast into 5 even slices and arrange on the greens. Spoon 6 tablespoons of the yellow tomato vinaigrette over the salad at the time of service.

Duckling Confit
Corn Relish and Wild Rice Potato Cakes
yield 4 servings

1 recipe Wild Rice Potato Cakes
(recipe on page 83)

Duck:
2 whole ducks (2½ pounds
each)
1½ teaspoons fresh thyme,
stemmed
3 tablespoons kosher salt
1 teaspoon cracked black pepper
1 bay leaf
2 tablespoons coarsely chopped
garlic
1 apple, cored, cut into 16
wedges

Corn Relish:
½ cup frozen corn, thawed
¼ cup diced red pepper, ¼-inch
dice
¼ cup diced red onion, ¼-inch
dice
¼ cup diced green pepper,
¼-inch dice
1 tablespoon chopped cilantro
1 teaspoon finely chopped
jalapeno* pepper
2 tablespoons olive oil
2 tablespoons lime juice
Salt to taste
Black pepper to taste
½ teaspoon finely chopped garlic

If you make this dish, you will have completed a basic culinary course and can hold your own when any conversation turns to cooking or food. It is a European classic, re-created with Midwestern influences by our chefs. If you are looking for a showstopper, look no more!

Remove the legs and breast from the duck carcass with a sharp knife. Trim all the available fat from the duck and place it in a heavy bottomed sauce pot. Over medium heat render out the duck fat and reserve it for later use. This can be done in advance.

Place the breast and legs in a stainless steel container and season with thyme, kosher salt, pepper, bay leaf, garlic, and apples. Store, chilled for 24 hours.

To prepare the confit, remove the legs only and place them in a sauce pot with the rendered duck fat and the apples, herbs, garlic and bay leaf. Bring to a simmer over medium heat and reduce to a low heat and cook for 1½ to 2 hours. The fat must cover the legs. If you need to, vegetable oil may be added to accomplish this. The duck legs should be tender to the touch and be easily separated from the bone when fully cooked. This recipe may be prepared to this stage 2-3 days in advance and refrigerated.

Place the breast skin side down in a heavy bottomed pan over medium heat. Allow to sear for 15 minutes until medium, or juices pool on top; remove. Slice the breast on the bias just before serving. The legs may be reheated by placing them in a pie pan and baking in a 375-degree oven for 20 minutes.

Photo on page 135

In a large bowl, combine corn, red pepper, onion, green pepper, cilantro, jalapeno pepper, olive oil, lime juice, salt, pepper, and garlic. Set aside.

After the duck legs have been heated through, place on the center of each plate. Spoon ¼ cup corn relish next to each duck leg. Arrange the breast slices on the leg in a fan-like pattern. Serve with Wild Rice Potato Cakes.

*Chef's Note: When handling hot peppers, avoid touching face and eyes. Wash hands thoroughly with warm, soapy water; rinse well.

Roast Duck
with Door County Cherry Sauce and Cinnamon Toasted Almonds

yield 4 servings

Duck:
- 2 ducklings (4-5 pounds each)
  Salt to taste
  Black pepper to taste
- 2 cups chicken broth
- ½ cup red wine

Sauce:
- 1 cup cranberry juice (divided)
- 2 cups chicken broth
- ½ cup red wine
- ½ cup dried Door County cherries
- 2 tablespoons packed brown sugar
- 1 tablespoon chopped onion
- 1 tablespoon raspberry jelly
- 1 teaspoon chopped garlic
- ¼ teaspoon poultry seasoning
  Salt to taste
  Black pepper to taste
- 2 tablespoons cornstarch

Almonds:
- ¼ cup slivered almonds
- 1 tablespoon melted butter
- 1 tablespoon sugar
- ½ teaspoon cinnamon

Dried Door County cherries add authentic Wisconsin regional flavor to the sauce that accompanies this roast duckling entree from River Wildlife. Toasted slivered almonds with a kiss of sugar and spice add just the right crunchy finish.

Cut ducks in half lengthwise; remove insides and rinse. Place duck halves in a greased baking dish. Season with desired amount of salt and pepper. Add chicken broth and red wine. Place in a preheated 400-degree oven and bake for 1 hour; reduce heat to 375-degrees and bake for another hour and 15 minutes. Prick skin every 20 minutes to release the fat. Remove from oven and pan and place on rack to drain.

Place ½ cup cranberry juice, broth, wine, cherries, sugar, onion, jelly, garlic, poultry seasoning, salt and pepper in 2-quart saucepan. Bring to boil; reduce to medium heat. Simmer for about 10 minutes. Combine remaining ½ cup cranberry juice and cornstarch; mix well to dissolve the cornstarch. Add to the simmering mixture; increase heat to high and bring to a boil, stirring constantly. When sauce is thickened, reduce heat to low and keep warm until ready to serve or remove from heat and reheat when duck is ready.

Toss almonds in melted butter. Mix sugar and cinnamon and sprinkle over almonds. Place in a preheated 375-degree oven and toast for about 15 minutes. Remove from oven and place on paper towel.

To serve, place duck half on each dinner plate. Top with ¼ of sauce and sprinkle with ¼ of toasted almonds. Serve with wild rice pilaf or starch of your choice.

Farm Raised Pheasant Breast

with Chardonnay Wine, White Grapes and Chanterelles, Warm Smoked Onions and Roasted Potato Salad

yield 4 servings

1 recipe Smoked Onion and
Roasted Potato Salad (recipe
on page 82)

Pheasant:
4 farm-raised pheasant breasts,
(8 ounces each) skin on,
boneless
Salt to taste
Black pepper to taste
¼ cup vegetable oil
½ cup chardonnay wine
2 cups Brown Chicken Stock
(see recipe on page 185)

Grapes and Chanterelles:
2 tablespoons butter (divided)
1 teaspoon stemmed, chopped
fresh thyme
½ cup chopped shallots
½ cup sliced fresh chanterelles
(canned chanterelles may
be used)
½ cup white seedless grapes, cut
in half lengthwise
½ cup Madeira wine
Salt to taste
Black pepper to taste
2 tablespoons chopped garlic
1 tablespoon fresh chives
1 pound fresh spinach, washed,
stems removed

This timeless classic with European influences was created for a special wedding celebration at The American Club by our Executive Chef, Rhys Lewis. Everything about this dish is memorable —and worthy of an encore performance.

Season the pheasant breasts with salt and pepper. In a hot 12-inch sauté pan, sauté the pheasant in the vegetable oil, until golden brown. Remove pheasant from sauté pan and put into an oven proof dish. Pour chardonnay wine and chicken stock on the pheasant and bake in a preheated 325-degree oven, uncovered, for approximately 7-10 minutes. Internal temperature should be 145 degrees. Reserve for service.

In another 12-inch sauté pan, melt 1 tablespoon butter and sauté the thyme, shallots, chanterelles and white grapes over medium heat. Add the Madeira wine and simmer gently. Pour in any juices from the baking dish and season to taste with salt and pepper. Take the remaining 1 tablespoon of butter and melt it in a sauté pan over medium heat. Add the garlic, chives and spinach; sauté lightly to wilt, but not enough to discolor it. Season to taste with salt and pepper.

Arrange the spinach in the center of four serving plates. Slice the breasts on an angle and fan out over the spinach. Spoon grapes and mushrooms on the pheasant; finish by pouring juices over pheasant. Serve surrounded with Smoked Onion and Roasted Potato Salad.

Oven Roasted Cornish Game Hens
Wild Mushrooms, Roasted Shallots and Natural Jus
yield 4 servings

Cornish Hens:
- 4 cornish hens (approximately 14 ounces each)
- ¼ cup vegetable oil
- 1 teaspoon stemmed, chopped fresh rosemary
- 1 teaspoon stemmed, chopped fresh thyme
- Salt to taste
- Black pepper to taste

Mushrooms, Shallots and Jus:
- ½ cup dried morel mushrooms
- ½ cup warm water
- 16 whole shallots, peeled
- 2 tablespoons butter
- ½ cup button mushrooms, cut in quarters
- ½ cup sliced fresh porcini mushrooms (can use dried if fresh are not available)
- 2 tablespoons chopped fresh garlic
- 1 cup chardonnay wine
- 4 cups Chicken Stock (see recipe on page 184)
- Salt to taste
- Black pepper to taste
- 1 tablespoon finely chopped chives
- 20 asparagus spears, for garnish
- 1 cup peeled, cut ⅛-inch dice, carrots, for garnish
- 4 sprigs fresh rosemary, for garnish

Cornish game hens make a charming plate presentation however they are prepared. But when they are perfectly oven-roasted and served up with a medley of mushrooms and bright green asparagus spears, they approach perfection.

Remove the giblets from the cornish hens and rinse with cold water. Tie legs together with string. Rub with oil, rosemary and thyme. Season with salt and pepper. Place in an oven proof 12-inch sauté pan and roast in a preheated 350-degree oven for 30 minutes, or until internal temperature is 140-degrees.

Meanwhile, to rehydrate dried morel mushrooms, place in warm water. (If using dried porcini mushrooms, rehydrate them in a separate ½ cup of warm water.) Set aside.

Remove hens from oven. With a French knife cut the back bone out, separate the legs and breasts with your fingers; remove other bones. Save bones for making jus. Reserve meat in a warm place.

Remove excess fat from sauté pan. Add shallots and return to preheated 350-degree oven for 10 minutes. Toss for even browning. Reserve.

In the same sauté pan, add butter, all mushrooms, garlic and chardonnay. Sauté until tender. Reserve.

In a sauce pan, reduce the chicken broth; add bones and reduce liquid until 1 cup remains. Add liquid to sauté pan with mushrooms. Season with salt, pepper and chives.

While broth is reducing, blanch asparagus spears. Cook carrots until tender, approximately 5-7 minutes.

To serve, place the two legs crossing each other in the center of the serving plate. Using a slotted spoon, top with one-fourth of the mushrooms. Place breast on top of mushrooms and spoon one-fourth of sauce over breast. Garnish with 5 asparagus spears, one-fourth of carrots and 4 shallots at 3 points of the plate. Tuck rosemary sprig under breast and serve.

Fish & Seafood

Seared Sea Scallops
with Red Oak and Endive and Great Lakes Caviar
yield 4 servings

Dressing:
- ¾ cup olive oil
- 2 teaspoons cracked black pepper
- 2½ tablespoons lemon juice
- 1 tablespoon stemmed, chopped fresh basil
- 1 teaspoon stemmed, chopped fresh thyme
- ½ teaspoon stemmed, chopped fresh rosemary
- 1 teaspoon ground coriander
- 1 tablespoon peeled, chopped garlic
- 1 teaspoon rice wine vinegar
- 5 medium tomatoes

Scallops:
- 24 sea scallops (10-20 count per pound)
  - Salt to taste
  - Black pepper to taste
  - Old Bay Seasoning to taste

Garnish:
- 4 leaves Belgian endive, split lengthwise
- 1 tablespoon chili powder
- 4 leaves red oak lettuce
- 4 teaspoons keta caviar
- 4 teaspoons golden caviar
- 4 teaspoons sturgeon caviar
- 20 sprigs fresh dill

Tender sea scallops are so quick and easy to cook. They make ideal entrees for busy cooks who want to practice their culinary skills. A lovely light dressing and a bit of caviar make this a memorable dish.

In a small bowl, blend olive oil, black pepper, lemon juice, basil, thyme, rosemary, coriander, garlic, and rice wine vinegar. Reserve. Peel, seed and dice tomatoes. Set aside.

Preheat a 12-inch heavy bottomed sauté pan to medium high heat. Season scallops with salt, pepper and Old Bay seasoning. Sear scallops dry in sauté pan, to a golden brown, approximately 3½ minutes on each side. Make sure you turn very *gently* to avoid tearing scallops.

Toss the diced tomatoes with ½ cup of the dressing; place ½ cup of the tomatoes in the center of each plate. Place six scallops around tomatoes. Dip the tips of endive in chili powder and insert with red oak leaf in the center of the tomatoes, so that it stands up. Place one teaspoon of each of the caviars at three points of the plate. Spoon some of the dressing over the scallops and garnish with 5 sprigs of fresh dill.

Grilled Sea Scallops and Shrimp
with Pineapple Salsa and Honey Lime Butter
yield 6 servings

1 recipe Pineapple Salsa (see recipe on page 173)

Butter:
1 lime
½ cup butter, room temperature
1 tablespoon honey
Dash cayenne pepper
1 tablespoon peeled, finely chopped shallots
Parchment paper or plastic wrap

Scallops and Shrimp:
12 bamboo skewers, soaked in water for 30 minutes
¼ cup vegetable oil
12 sea scallops (10-12 count)
12 large shrimp (13-15 count), peeled and deveined
Salt to taste
Black pepper to taste
Cilantro leaves (optional), for garnish

Pretty pink and white seafood team with a colorful fruit and vegetable salsa to form the base ingredients for a hot weather supper entree. This cooks quickly on the grill, so keep a close watch to guarantee a tender, tasty dish.

Grate zest (outer green layer) from lime. Squeeze juice from lime. (You should get 1 teaspoon zest and ¼ cup juice.)

In food processor or with a hand mixer, combine butter, lime zest and juice, honey, cayenne pepper, and shallots. Mix until well blended. Spoon the soft butter to the center of parchment paper and roll into a log. Refrigerate for 3 hours or until firm. To serve, slice the butter in ⅛-inch slices.

To prepare scallops and shrimp, put vegetable oil in a small bowl. Toss scallops and shrimp in oil to coat. Place one scallop in the center of each shrimp and double skewer with bamboo skewers. Season to taste with salt and pepper. Trim off skewers, leaving at least an inch on each end.

On a preheated outdoor grill or grill pan, grill the seafood brochettes until grill marks form and shrimp and scallops are opaque. Be careful not to overcook.

Spoon the pineapple salsa on the center of the serving plate. While holding the seafood brochette with your hand, remove skewers. Arrange two seafood brochettes on pineapple salsa.

While still hot, lay sliced honey lime butter on seafood brochettes to melt; garnish with cilantro leaves and serve.

Linguine with Grilled Gulf Shrimp
Dried Tomatoes and Wilted Spinach
yield 4 servings

½ pound linguine pasta, dry weight
¾ cup olive oil (divided)
1½ cups dried tomatoes
1 cup hot water
16 shrimp (10-15 count), peeled and deveined
   Salt to taste
   Black pepper to taste
¼ cup peeled, chopped garlic
2 pounds leaf spinach, stemmed, washed
¼ cup Madeira wine
1 cup washed, stemmed, chopped fresh basil leaves
2 tablespoons washed, stemmed, chopped fresh thyme leaves
1 cup grated Wisconsin Asiago cheese
1 cup grated Wisconsin Parmesan cheese

Cucina's most popular pasta dish can be re-created in your own kitchen. Grilled shrimp, fresh spinach and a delightful blend of Wisconsin cheeses make this an eclectic favorite.

Cook the linguine in a large pot of salted boiling water until al dente. Drain. Toss with ¼ cup of the olive oil and reserve.

In a small bowl, combine dried tomatoes with water. Set aside and let soak for at least ½ hour.

Preheat an outdoor grill or grill pan.

Season shrimp with salt and pepper, rub with 2 tablespoons olive oil and grill 2-3 minutes until cooked. Reserve.

Preheat a 12-inch sauté pan. Pour in remaining 6 tablespoons olive oil and reserved shrimp, add garlic and toss lightly. Add leaf spinach and toss so it begins to wilt. Add reserved linguine, Madeira wine, basil, thyme, dried tomatoes, and liquid. Allow the pasta to cook over medium heat to absorb the liquids. Season to taste with salt and pepper.

Portion onto serving plates and top with Asiago and Parmesan cheeses.

Fillet of Norwegian Salmon
Tomato, Cucumber Salad and Potato Crisps
yield 4 servings

Potato Crisps:
- 2 baking potatoes (8 ounces) sliced paper thin
- 2 sweet potatoes (8 ounces) sliced paper thin
- Vegetable oil, for frying
- Salt to taste
- Cayenne pepper to taste

Herb Oil:
- 1 small bunch (approximately 1 cup) fresh dill
- 1 shallot, peeled
- 4 cloves garlic, peeled
- 1 cup vegetable oil
- 1 cup olive oil
- 2 teaspoons kosher salt
- 2 teaspoons cracked black pepper

Tomato, Cucumber Salad:
- 1 small red onion, julienne
- 1 beefsteak tomato, julienne (chop inside for garnish)
- 1 English (seedless) cucumber, julienne green part only
- 1 small red pepper, julienne
- 3 tablespoons olive oil
- 4 tablespoons rice wine vinegar
- 2 teaspoons chopped fresh dill
- 1 teaspoon kosher salt
- 1 teaspoon cracked black pepper
- 1 radicchio cup, for garnish

Salmon:
- 3 tablespoons whole mustard seed
- 1 tablespoon five peppercorn blend
- 4 salmon fillets (6 ounces each)
- 2 tablespoons vegetable oil (divided)

Peppercorn-crusted salmon coupled with homemade potato crisps, and a cool, colorful salad create a beautiful plate. Keep this recipe in mind when the occasion calls for something special.

Rinse potatoes in cold water; let drain thoroughly. In a preheated 350-degree deep fat fryer, fry potatoes until lightly brown, about 2 minutes. When finished, place on paper towels and season with salt and pepper. Reserve at room temperature.

In a food processor, combine dill, shallots and garlic; process until finely chopped. Add oils, season with salt and pepper; blend and reserve.

In a medium bowl, combine onion, tomato, cucumber and pepper. Add oil, vinegar, dill, salt and pepper. Toss lightly to combine; reserve.

In a blender, combine mustard seeds and peppercorn blend. Blend until coarsely crushed; reserve. Brush salmon on both sides with reserved herb oil. Bread one side of salmon with reserved peppercorn blend. In a 12-inch sauté pan, add 1 tablespoon oil and heat to very hot. Pan sear salmon approximately 45 seconds to 1 minute on each side. Use remaining oil to coat cookie sheet. Remove salmon from pan and place on cookie sheet. Finish in a preheated 325-degree oven for approximately 3 minutes.

Place radicchio cup on serving plate and place 1/3 cup of the salad in cup. Place 1 cup of the potato crisps on plate. Lean salmon fillet on salad and chips. Spoon 2 tablespoons of herb oil on plate and finish with chopped tomato. Serve.

Photo on page 70

Chilled Atlantic Salmon
Thai Vinaigrette, Asparagus and Yellow Tomatoes
yield 4 servings

Salmon:
- 2 tablespoons finely chopped fresh chives
- 2 tablespoons stemmed, chopped fresh thyme
- Kosher salt to taste
- Cracked black pepper to taste
- 4 salmon fillets (6 ounces each)
- ¼ cup vegetable oil

Wontons:
- 2 cups vegetable oil
- 8 wonton skins, cut into ⅛-inch strips

Vegetables:
- 1 cup julienne cut tomatoes
- ½ pint yellow teardrop tomatoes
- 12 asparagus spears

Dressing:
- ¾ cup olive oil
- ¼ cup Pommeray vinegar
- 2 tablespoons finely chopped chives
- ¼ cup orange juice
- ½ teaspoon cracked black peppercorns
- 1 teaspoon lemon zest
- 2 teaspoons minced candied ginger
- 2 teaspoons Thai red curry base

Here's a chilled salmon entree that borrows from Thai cooking for some of its flavors and ingredients. If you enjoy serving entrees that excite the taste buds, you will want to add this to your recipe repertoire.

In a small bowl, combine chives, thyme, salt and pepper. Pat seasonings on salmon fillets.

Heat a 12-inch sauté pan to medium high heat, add the oil and place the salmon in pan. Sear until golden brown on both sides. Finish in a preheated 350-degree oven for 5 minutes. Reserve covered in the refrigerator.

To prepare wontons, heat the oil to 350 degrees, in a small sauce pan. Fry the wontons, stirring lightly with a fork until crisp. Remove and drain on paper towels.

Cut teardrop tomatoes in half. Blanch asparagus spears and slice on bias. Set vegetables aside.

Combine olive oil, vinegar, chives, orange juice, peppercorns, lemon zest, ginger, and red curry base in a blender. Blend well.

Toss tomatoes and asparagus in the dressing; place in the center of the serving plate. Slice the salmon portions into three pieces and arrange on the vegetables. Spoon dressing over salmon and garnish with reserved wonton skins.

Pan Seared Salmon
Smokehouse Almond Butter
yield 4 servings

Almond Butter:
- 3 ounces Smokehouse almonds
- ½ cup butter, softened
- 1 scallion, sliced
- ¼ teaspoon lemon zest
- ¼ teaspoon chopped garlic
- ¼ teaspoon ground black pepper
- ¼ teaspoon salt, or to taste

Salmon:
- 4 salmon fillets (8 ounces each), skinless, boneless
- Cooking spray
- Morton's Nature's Seasoning or seasoning of your choice

From the kitchens of River Wildlife, our 500-acre wilderness preserve, comes this creation of delicate salmon delightfully countered with a smoke-flavored almond butter. You will enjoy the contrast in flavors.

Place almonds in a food processor and coarsely chop. Add butter, scallion, lemon zest, garlic, black pepper and salt. Mix thoroughly. Chill until ready to use.

To pan sear salmon, heat a 12-inch sauté pan or frying pan on high until a few drops of water sizzle in bottom of pan. Spray with cooking spray and place salmon in pan and sear each side for about 45 seconds. Sprinkle with seasoning; remove and place on baking sheet that has been sprayed with vegetable oil spray. Bake in a preheated 350-degree oven with or without Almond Butter* for about 12-15 minutes or until fish is flaky but still moist. Can also be baked with a few teaspoons of fresh lemon juice and or white wine.

*Chef's Note: This butter can be placed on salmon before baking if desired (about 1 tablespoon per serving), or can be served on the side.

Pan Seared Walleye
English Cucumber Salad and Crisp Fried Potatoes
yield 4 servings

Cucumber Salad:
- 2 cups peeled, julienne cut English cucumbers
- ½ cup skinned, seeded, julienne cut, tomatoes
- ¾ cup Spa English Cucumber and Dill Dressing (see recipe on page 57)

Walleye:
- ¼ cup olive oil
- 4 walleye portions (6 ounces each)
  Kosher salt to taste
  Black pepper to taste
- 2 tablespoons chopped dill

Potatoes:
- 3 baking potatoes
- 4 cups vegetable oil
- 1 teaspoon kosher salt
- ½ teaspoon Old Bay seasoning

Crisp, cool and slightly smokey textures and tastes come together in this clever melange of fish, vegetable and salad. We like to think that this is a perfect summertime entree.

In a large bowl, toss the cucumbers and tomatoes lightly in the Spa English Cucumber and Dill Dressing. Set aside.

To prepare walleye, preheat a 10-inch sauté pan over medium heat; add the olive oil. Season the fillets with salt, pepper and dill. Brown lightly, flesh side down and reserve.

Peel potatoes and slice ¹⁄₁₆-inch thick. Heat the vegetable oil in a large sauce pot to 325 degrees. Cook the potatoes in the hot oil until they are golden brown and crisp. Season with salt and Old Bay seasoning.

To serve, place one-fourth of the potato crisps on a serving plate. Lay the walleye fillet on the potatoes and lay one-fourth of the cucumber salad over the edge of the walleye and serve.

Seared Fillet of Fresh Walleye
with Toasted Sesame Crust
yield 6 servings

Marinade:
- ½ cup soy sauce
- ¼ cup rice wine vinegar
- 2 tablespoons sesame oil
- 2 tablespoons vegetable oil
- 2 tablespoons horseradish
- 2 tablespoons honey
- 1 teaspoon peeled, chopped garlic

Vegetables:
- ½ cup julienne cut pea pods, stemmed
- ½ cup julienne cut Chinese cabbage
- ½ cup peeled, julienne cut cucumber
- ½ cup julienne cut red onion
- ½ cup julienne cut red pepper
- 12 red oak leaves, washed, for garnish
- 6 endive spears, split, for garnish

Walleye:
- 2¼ pounds walleye fillets, cut into 6 portions (6 ounces each), skin removed
- Salt to taste
- Black pepper to taste
- ½ cup honey mustard
- ½ cup sesame seeds
- 1 tablespoon black sesame seeds
- ½ cup vegetable oil

A Great Lakes favorite takes on an Oriental twist in this delightful departure of traditional food flavors. Even the vegetables get into the act and suggest a bit of the Pacific Rim. Remember this dish if you prefer fish in a lighter presentation.

In a small bowl, combine soy sauce, vinegar, sesame oil, vegetable oil, horseradish, honey, and garlic. Mix well.

In a large bowl, toss pea pods, cabbage, cucumber, red onion, and red pepper in marinade. Set aside.

Season walleye with salt and pepper; brush with honey mustard; coat with sesame seeds and black sesame seeds.

Preheat a heavy bottomed 12-inch sauté pan over medium high heat. Add vegetable oil; sear the walleye fillets until the sesame seeds are golden brown. Finish in the oven at 325 degrees, if necessary, until fish flakes easily with fork.

Arrange one-sixth of vegetables in the center of each serving plate; slice each 6 ounce portion of the walleye fillets in half and place them on the salad to the front of the plate. Place two leaves of oak leaf and split endive leaf in the center of the vegetables for garnish. Serve.

Photo on page 69

Freshwater Crayfish Ravioli
Pesto Cream and Roasted Tomatoes
yield 4 servings

Herb Oil:
- 2 teaspoons stemmed, finely chopped fresh basil
- 1 teaspoon stemmed, finely chopped fresh thyme
- 1 teaspoon stemmed, finely chopped fresh rosemary
- 2 teaspoons finely chopped garlic
- 1 cup vegetable oil

Roasted Tomatoes:
- 5 tomatoes
- 2 tablespoons herb oil

Crayfish Filling:
- 1 tablespoon butter
- 1 tablespoon finely chopped garlic
- 3 tablespoons finely chopped scallions
- 4 dashes hot sauce
- ¼ pound finely chopped, cooked crayfish
- 2 cups grated Wisconsin Asiago cheese

Pasta Dough:
- ½ cup semolina flour
- 1½ cups all-purpose flour
- 5 large eggs (divided)
- Extra all-purpose flour for kneading
- Extra semolina flour for dusting
- 1 tablespoon water

Pesto Cream:
- ¼ cup basil pesto (see recipe on page 171)
- ½ cup heavy whipping cream
- ½ teaspoon finely chopped fresh garlic

While this dish has a number of steps, much of the work can be done in advance. The final preparations are extremely simple and can be completed in the company of your guests. The flavors are absolutely wonderful.

In a small bowl, combine basil, thyme, rosemary, garlic, and oil. Mix well. Reserve.

Peel and seed tomatoes; coarsely chop. In ovenproof dish, toss tomatoes with herb oil. Place in a preheated 350-degree oven for 10-15 minutes or until oil is absorbed. Remove from oven. Set aside.

To make crayfish fillings, melt butter in 12-inch sauté pan. Add garlic, scallions and sauté until tender. Add hot sauce and crayfish, mix well. Stir in cheese and remove from heat. Chill, covered in refrigerator until use.

To prepare pasta dough, sift both flours onto flat surface and make a well in the center. Beat 4 eggs and pour into well. With fingertips, mix together until the dough is soft and begins to stick together. When the dough comes together, knead dough with heal of hand for 10-15 minutes. Set aside and let rest for 1 hour.

Roll out dough and place in pasta machine on lowest numerical setting, working the dough thinner each time until it is approximately ¹⁄₁₆-inch thick.

Dust pasta dough with semolina flour to prevent sticking. Lay pasta dough sheet out. Cut into forty 2½-inch diameter circles. Combine remaining egg and water; beat well to make an egg wash. Brush all dough circles with egg wash.

Place one teaspoon of crayfish filling on twenty of the circles. Cover with remaining twenty circles. Gently press edges together. In a large pot of boiling water, add ravioli; reduce to simmer; cook for 4 minutes. Remove from water. Drain. Makes 20 ravioli.

Combine pesto, cream and garlic in a 10-inch sauté pan. Bring to a boil; allow to thicken slightly. Remove from heat and keep warm.

Pool 3 tablespoons of basil pesto on each serving plate.

Arrange 5 ravioli overlapping in a circle on center of plate.

Place ¼ cup roasted tomatoes in the middle of ravioli and at three points of the plate.

Drizzle remaining basil pesto over plate for garnish.

Pecan Crusted Rainbow Trout
with Citrus Salad
yield 4 servings

Salad:
- 1 orange
- 1 lemon
- 2 grapefruit
- 1 tomato, julienne cut
- 1 julienne cut English cucumber (½ cup)
- ½ cup julienne cut red onion
- ¼ cup basil leaves, cut into thin strips
- 1 tablespoon minced chives
- 1 tablespoon minced crystallized ginger
- ½ teaspoon chopped garlic
- ⅛ cup rice wine vinegar
- ¼ cup olive oil
  - Salt to taste
  - Black pepper to taste
- 14 radicchio leaves

Herbed Bread Crumbs:
- 1 cup dried regular bread crumbs
- 1½ teaspoons dried leaf thyme
- 1 teaspoon dried leaf rosemary
- 2 tablespoons minced chives
- 1½ teaspoons chopped garlic
- ½ teaspoon coriander
- 4½ teaspoons mustard seed, finely ground in blender
  - Salt to taste
  - Black pepper to taste

Rainbow Trout:
- ½ cup finely chopped pecans
- 4 rainbow trout fillets (1 pound each), cleaned, skinned
  - Salt to season
  - Black pepper to season
- 1 cup buttermilk
- 2 tablespoons vegetable oil

Fresh rainbow trout is a treat in itself, but when teamed with a crunchy breading and accompanied by a colorful citrus salad, it is exquisite.

Peel orange, lemon and grapefruit; divide into segments and combine in large bowl. Add tomatoes, cucumbers, red onion, basil leaves, chives, ginger, garlic, rice wine vinegar, olive oil, and salt and pepper to taste. Set aside.

To make herbed bread crumbs, combine regular bread crumbs, thyme, rosemary, chives, garlic, coriander, and mustard seed. Season with salt and pepper.

Combine bread crumbs and pecans; set aside. Season trout with salt and pepper; dip in buttermilk, then press one side only in crumbs.

In a large heavy bottomed frying pan, heat vegetable oil and pan sear both sides of fish until golden brown and cooked through, about 3 to 4 minutes on each side. Keep warm.

Arrange the radicchio leaves together to form a cup using four radicchio leaves. Place radicchio cups in the center of each serving plate. Spoon one-fourth of citrus salad into each radicchio cup. Slice rainbow trout fillets in half width wise, arrange in an "X" pattern on the citrus salad and serve.

Mixed Grill of Fresh Water Fish
Country Dijon Butter Sauce,
Mushroom, Scallion and Wild Rice Blend,
Pea Pods and Shiitake Mushrooms
yield 4 servings

1 recipe Mushroom, Scallion and Wild Rice Blend (see recipe on page 79)

Fish:
 ¾ pound lake perch fillets, skinless, boneless
 ¾ pound brook trout fillets, skinless, boneless
 ¾ pound walleye fillets, skinless, boneless
 2 tablespoons vegetable oil
 Salt to taste
 Black pepper to taste

Butter Sauce:
 ½ cup chardonnay wine
 1 tablespoon lemon juice
 1 tablespoon peeled, finely chopped shallots
 1 bay leaf
 ½ teaspoon chopped fresh garlic
 ¼ pound lightly salted butter, chilled well, cut in small pieces
 ¼ cup heavy whipping cream
 1 tablespoon country style-Dijon mustard
 1 tablespoon minced chives, for garnish

Vegetables:
 6 shiitake mushrooms, about 2 inches in diameter
 1 leek
 1 tablespoon butter
 1 tablespoon peeled, chopped shallots
 1 cup pea pods, stems removed
 1 cup julienne cut red pepper

This is our taster's medley for guests who just can't decide which fish to order. The accompanying Dijon Butter Sauce adds a flavor fillip as do the Far Eastern vegetables.

Preheat an outdoor charcoal grill. Cut each fillet into 4 pieces. Coat fish with oil; season with salt and pepper. Grill on hot grill lightly, approximately 2-3 minutes on each side; do not overcook. Reserve in a warm oven.

In a heavy bottomed sauce pot, put the wine, lemon juice, shallots, bay leaf, and garlic. Simmer until the liquid reduces to ¼ cup. Whip in the butter (a piece at a time) and heavy cream with a wire whisk until blended. Add the mustard and remove the bay leaf. Reserve the sauce in a warm place.

Remove and discard stems from mushrooms; cut tops in ¼-inch wide strips. Cut leek in julienne. Melt the butter in a sauté pan and add the shallots; sauté the pea pods, red peppers, shiitake mushrooms and leeks until tender crisp.

In the center of a plate, place a timbale of the Mushroom, Scallion and Wild Rice Blend (approximately ½ cup). Place about a tablespoon of the vegetables at three points of the plate and place on each, one piece of each of the fresh water fish. Spoon each fish with a tablespoon of the butter sauce. Sprinkle with chives and serve.

Meats

Pan Grilled Mignon of Kohler PureLean™ Beef

with Grilled Vegetables

yield 6 servings

Marinade:
- Salt to taste
- Black pepper to taste
- 1 teaspoon chopped fresh garlic
- 1 teaspoon chopped fresh rosemary
- 1 teaspoon chopped fresh thyme
- ½ cup vegetable oil

Mignon and Vegetables:
- 6 Kohler PureLean™ Beef mignons (6 ounces each) or a high quality beef
- 18 red bliss potatoes
- 1 8-inch zucchini, cut in ⅓-inch bias slices
- 1 8-inch summer squash, cut in ⅓-inch bias slices
- 2 red peppers, cut in julienne
- 2 green peppers, cut in julienne
- 18 scallions, tops removed
- Salt to taste
- Black pepper to taste

Less fat in our PureLean Beef makes it a perfect choice for cooks who are health conscious. A fresh herb-based marinade enriches the satisfying taste of beef and the accompanying grilled vegetables.

Whisk together marinade ingredients. In one-half of the mixture, marinate the beef mignons for 24 hours in refrigerator. Reserve other half for later use.

Parboil red bliss potatoes; cut in half. Set aside.

Heat an outdoor grill or grill pan as hot as possible before starting (be sure to have adequate ventilation when using grill pan inside because it will generate smoke). Grill the mignons, marking each side with crisscross marks; reserve in a warm spot.

Toss zucchini, summer squash, red and green peppers, scallions, and potatoes in the remaining marinade and grill in the pan, marking each side with crisscross marks. Remove to a cookie sheet and keep warm until all vegetables are done. Arrange the vegetables in a pattern on the plate and set mignon in the center.

Photo on page 136

Mustard and Herb Crusted Sirloin of Kohler PureLean™ Beef

yield 6 servings

Marinade:
- Salt to taste
- Black pepper to taste
- 1 teaspoon chopped fresh garlic
- 1 teaspoon chopped fresh rosemary
- 1 teaspoon chopped fresh thyme
- ½ cup vegetable oil
- 6 Kohler PureLean™ sirloin steaks (9 ounces each) or high quality steaks

Herb Crust:
- 2 cups dried plain bread crumbs
- 1 tablespoon chopped, stemmed fresh thyme
- 2 teaspoons chopped, stemmed fresh rosemary
- ¼ cup chives
- 1 tablespoon chopped garlic
- 1 teaspoon coriander
- 3 tablespoons mustard seed, well ground in blender
- Salt to taste
- Black pepper to taste
- 1 large egg
- 8 ounces honey mustard

Accompaniments:
- 2 pounds fresh leaf spinach, stemmed, washed
- ½ head of savoy cabbage
- 1 tablespoon peeled, finely chopped shallots
- 1 tablespoon unsalted butter
- Salt to taste
- Black pepper to taste
- Vegetable oil
- 5 baking potatoes, peeled and sliced ¹⁄₁₆-inch

The secret to this well-seasoned, tender entree is in the marinade ingredients. The flavorful herb crust encases pre-grilled steaks in just the right taste package.

Whisk together marinade ingredients. Marinate sirloin steak for 24 hours in refrigerator.

Preheat an outdoor grill or grill pan.

In a large bowl, combine bread crumbs with thyme, rosemary, chives, garlic, coriander, and mustard seed. Season to taste with salt and pepper. Set aside.

In small bowl, whip egg until frothy; mix in honey mustard. Set aside.

Sear the sirloin steaks on the grill until done medium rare. Remove from grill; brush with the honey mustard mixture and dip in the bread crumbs. Brown in a preheated 350-degree oven until golden, for approximately 4-5 minutes (internal temperature should reach 140 degrees); do not overcook.

Wilt the spinach and savoy cabbage in boiling water; drain and toss with shallots. Season with butter, salt and pepper. Set aside in warm place.

In a large frying pan, fry sliced potatoes in oil until crisp; season to taste.

To serve, arrange the wilted greens in the center of the plate. Slice sirloin on bias in thin pieces and fan it out on the front of the plate. Arrange the potatoes on the rear of the plate and serve.

Herb-Crusted Tenderloin of Beef
Two Tomato and Grilled Onion Salad
Roasted Garlic Sauce
yield 4 servings

Garlic Sauce:
- 2 medium heads garlic, tops trimmed ¼-inch
- 1½ cups heavy whipping cream
- 1 tablespoon minced chives
- Salt to taste
- Black pepper to taste

Beef:
- 2 teaspoons chopped fresh thyme
- 1 teaspoon chopped fresh rosemary
- 2 teaspoons kosher salt
- 1 teaspoon cracked black pepper
- 1 teaspoon finely chopped fresh garlic
- 1½ pounds beef tenderloin
- 12 spears asparagus, blanched, for garnish

Salad:
- ¼ cup olive oil (divided)
- 1 medium Bermuda onion sliced ¼-inch thick
- ½ pint cherry tomatoes, cut in half
- ½ pint yellow teardrop tomatoes, cut in half
- 2 tablespoons chopped fresh basil
- 1 teaspoon chopped garlic
- Salt to taste
- Black pepper to taste

Roasting garlic tames its wilder nature and adds a sweet, nut-like flavor to the cloves. The addition of fresh herbs, garden-fresh tomatoes and asparagus make this an excellent summer entertaining entree.

Place garlic in a small baking dish. Bake in a preheated 350-degree oven for approximately 45 minutes to 1 hour. Remove garlic from oven. Peel cloves and place in a sauté pan, add cream and reduce over high heat until the cream begins to thicken. Add chives, salt and pepper. Reserve.

To prepare beef, combine thyme, rosemary, kosher salt, pepper, and garlic in a small bowl. Rub herb mixture over beef tenderloin. Grill tenderloin quickly on preheated grill 2-3 minutes on each side. Place tenderloin in a 10-inch oven-proof sauté pan and finish roasting in a 350-degree oven, approximately 20 minutes or until internal temperature has reached 140-degrees. Remove tenderloin from sauté pan. Keep warm.

For salad, rub a small amount of oil on the onions and grill lightly, 3-4 minutes on each side.

In a medium bowl, toss the onions, cherry and yellow tomatoes, basil and garlic. Season with salt and pepper.

Place a half cup of the salad in the center of each plate. Slice the tenderloin into ¼-inch slices and fan on top of the salad. Place 3 asparagus spears at three points of the plate. Spoon 3 tablespoons of the roasted garlic sauce at three points of the plate. Serve.

Fillet of Kohler PureLean™ Beef
with Bean Melange and Three Tomato Salsa
yield 6 servings

1 recipe Three Tomato Salsa (see recipe on page 172)

Marinade:
1 teaspoon fresh garlic
1 teaspoon fresh rosemary
1 teaspoon fresh thyme
½ cup vegetable oil
  Salt to taste
  Black pepper to taste
6 Kohler PureLean™ Beef fillets (6 ounces each) or high quality fillets

Bean Melange:
1 cup pinto beans
1 cup black beans
1 cup kidney beans
3 teaspoons salt (divided)
3 dashes black pepper (divided)
6 teaspoons chopped garlic (divided)
2 tablespoons peanut oil
¼ cup olive oil
  Dash cayenne pepper
1 tablespoon chili powder
¼ teaspoon cumin
2 cups beef stock or bouillon

Onions:
½ cup flour
1 tablespoon chili powder
1 medium onion, sliced in rings
3 cups vegetable oil

Add south-of-the-border flare to your next beef fillet by incorporating beans, cilantro, peppers and lime into the recipe. These popular flavors will linger pleasantly on the palate.

To make marinade, chop the fresh herbs and add to the oil; season with salt and pepper. Marinate the fillets in refrigerator for 24 hours.

Cook beans separately (to retain color) in water seasoned with 1 tablespoon salt, a dash of pepper and 2 teaspoons garlic. Drain. In a large frying pan, combine beans and sauté in peanut and olive oil with the cayenne pepper, chili powder and cumin. Add beef stock to the beans; reduce liquid by half. Set aside in warm place.

Grill the fillets on a preheated outdoor grill until medium rare or to desired doneness.

Prepare onions by combining flour and chili powder in large bowl. Dredge the finely sliced onions in flour mixture and fry in hot oil until golden brown. Stir with a fork to prevent sticking together.

To serve, spoon the hot beans in the center of serving plate and set a fillet on them. Spoon the salsa around the fillet in three points of a triangle. Top the fillet with crisp fried onions and serve.

Big Sky Sub Sandwich

yield 4 servings

Beef Marinade:
¼ cup vegetable oil
2 tablespoons chili powder
¼ teaspoon ground white pepper
½ cup strong coffee
2 teaspoons peeled, finely chopped garlic
1 tablespoon lime juice
2 tablespoons cumin
1 tablespoon packed brown sugar
Salt to taste
Black pepper to taste
1 pound flank steak

Sandwich:
¼ cup vegetable oil
1 medium red pepper, cut julienne
1 medium green pepper, cut julienne
1 medium red onion, cut julienne
8 6-inch diameter flour tortillas
2 avocadoes, peeled, seeded, sliced into ⅛-inch wedges
1 recipe Three Tomato Salsa (see recipe on page 172)

Sour Cream:
1½ cups sour cream
2 teaspoons ground cumin
1 tablespoon lime juice
Salt to taste
Black pepper to taste

This hearty sandwich has a unique wrapper—tortillas instead of bread. You will like the pleasant departure from typical sub sandwich fillings that this recipe uses. Do serve it with the complementary Smoked Onion and Black Bean Soup (recipe on page 27).

In a medium bowl, combine oil, chili powder, white pepper, strong coffee, garlic, lime juice, cumin, brown sugar, salt and pepper; blend well. Marinate the flank steak for 24 hours in marinade.

Preheat an outdoor grill. Drain steak, reserving marinade. Grill steak, turning regularly and basting well with the marinade. Remove steak from grill when internal temperature is 140 degrees; reserve.

Heat a 10-inch sauté pan to medium heat and add oil, peppers and onions. Sauté 2-3 minutes; remove from heat and reserve.

In a small bowl, combine sour cream, cumin and lime juice. Season with salt and pepper; reserve.

Lay out the flour tortillas and spread each with 2 tablespoons of sour cream mixture. Portion the peppers and onions evenly on the tortillas. Slice flank steak on the bias, ⅛-inch thick. Evenly portion the flank steak among the flour tortillas. Place 3-4 slices of the avocado on each tortilla. Fold sides of the tortilla towards the center and secure it with a toothpick. Place two tortillas on each plate and serve with Three Tomato Salsa.

Tiger Meat Sandwich

yield 4 servings

4 ounces unsalted butter

8 slices dark rye bread

1 pound Kohler PureLean™ Beef (Ground Round) raw or a high quality beef

16 slices Spanish onions, ¼-inch thick

1 cup sliced dill pickles
    Salt to taste
    Black pepper to taste

4 ounces hot Dusseldorf mustard

1 recipe The American Club Red Bliss Potato Salad (see recipe on page 55)

In the 1940's, this sandwich was served at parties in the Tap Room (now known as The Horse & Plow Restaurant). We brought it back to our current menu and serve it with a shorty beer for the guest who likes a bit of gusto.

Spread butter evenly on four slices of bread. Divide raw beef into four equal portions; shape into round patties and place on the four slices of bread. Arrange onions and pickles on top of patty; season with salt and pepper. Spread mustard on remaining four slices of bread.

Place sandwich on serving plate; lay the mustard-covered bread next to it. Serve with The American Club Red Bliss Potato Salad.

Wood-Fired Loin of Venison
Barbecue Vinaigrette, Grilled Potato Salad, Marinated Cucumber, Red Onion and Tomatoes

yield 4 servings

Barbecue Rub and Venison:
- 1 tablespoon kosher salt
- 1 tablespoon ground black pepper
- 1 tablespoon packed brown sugar
- 1 tablespoon Barbecue seasoning
- 4 venison loins (4 ounces each) skinless, boneless
- 1 cup hickory chips, soaked in water for 24 hours

Barbecue Vinaigrette:
- ¼ cup strong coffee
- 2 tablespoons packed brown sugar
- 1 tablespoon liquid smoke
- Kosher salt to taste
- Black pepper to taste
- ½ teaspoon garlic powder
- 1 teaspoon chili powder
- ¼ cup rice wine vinegar
- 2 tablespoons ketchup
- ¼ cup vegetable oil

Vegetables:
- 1 cup peeled, julienne cut cucumber
- 1 cup julienne cut tomatoes
- 1 cup julienne cut Bermuda onion
- 2 tablespoons vegetable oil
- 2 tablespoons rice wine vinegar
- 2 tablespoons minced fresh chives
- Kosher salt to taste
- Black pepper to taste
- 8 leaves red oak lettuce
- 4 leaves green oak lettuce

Potato Salad:
- ½ pound or 6 red bliss potatoes, skin on
- 2 tablespoons vegetable oil
- Kosher salt to taste
- Black pepper to taste

Barbecue flavors double up, first as a dry spice "rub" and then in the barbecue-flavored vinaigrette that completes the presentation. Hickory chips add wonderful smokey flavors to this entree sure to be treasured by sportsmen and cooks who enjoy game dishes.

In a small bowl, combine kosher salt, black pepper, brown sugar and Barbecue seasoning. Rub mixture on the outside of the venison. This can be done in advance and then refrigerated.

To make vinaigrette, combine in a blender, strong coffee, brown sugar, liquid smoke, kosher salt, black pepper, garlic powder, chili powder, vinegar, ketchup, and oil. Blend until smooth. Set aside.

Toss the cucumbers, tomatoes and onions in oil, vinegar and chives. Season with kosher salt and pepper and reserve. Wash lettuce leaves and reserve for garnish.

In a 2-quart pot, place whole potatoes in 1 quart of cold water and bring to boil; cook until tender, but not falling apart, approximately 15 minutes. Remove the potatoes from the water and allow to cool. Cut them in half and toss lightly with vegetable oil; season with kosher salt and black pepper. Grill on preheated hot outdoor grill until grill marks develop. Remove the potatoes from grill; cut into quarters and reserve.

Reduce heat of grill and toss hickory chips onto the coals. Place the venison on the grill and turn frequently; cook rare to medium rare, approximately 3-4 minutes.

Photo on page 68

To serve, arrange one-fourth of the potatoes in the center of each plate. Slice each venison portion into ¼-inch thick slices and fan in a circle on top of the potatoes. Arrange one-fourth of greens in the center of the venison so that they stand up. Place one-fourth of cucumbers, onion and tomatoes around edge of each plate. Spoon the vinaigrette over the venison and serve.

Pine Nut Crusted Rack of Lamb
Wisconsin Gorgonzola Herb Cream,
Warm Salad of French Beans, and Potato
and Pear Flan
yield 4 servings

1 recipe Potato and Pear Flan
(see recipe on page 85)

Lamb Rack:
2 lamb racks (1½ pounds each),
Frenched
Salt to taste
Black pepper to taste
¼ cup honey mustard
3 tablespoons whole pine nuts
¼ cup dry bread crumbs
1 teaspoon finely chopped garlic
1 teaspoon finely chopped mint

Sauce:
2 tablespoons butter
2 tablespoons finely chopped
garlic
¼ cup peeled, finely chopped
shallots
1 cup heavy whipping cream
1 cup crumbled Wisconsin
Gorgonzola cheese
½ teaspoon Dijon-style mustard
½ teaspoon cracked black pepper
2 teaspoons stemmed, finely
chopped fresh oregano
2 tablespoons stemmed, finely
chopped fresh basil
½ teaspoon stemmed, finely
chopped fresh rosemary

Rack of lamb is always a spectacular presentation but our chefs have made it even better. Consider the addition of a flavorful breading for the lamb, a mild blue cheese sauce, and warm salad of fresh string beans, shiitake mushrooms and plum tomatoes. It's a must for the educated palate.

To French lamb rack: have the excess fat from racks removed by the meat butcher or remove the excess fat yourself. Season the racks with salt and pepper and grill on a preheated outdoor grill, or roast in a preheated 350-degree oven. The bones may brown too much so they may be covered with aluminum foil before starting, if desired. Cook until 100-degree internal temperature is reached. Rub the rack with the honey mustard. Set aside.

Toast the pine nuts on a baking sheet in a preheated 350-degree oven. Toast for approximately 10-15 minutes or until golden brown; watch closely not to burn. Remove from oven and allow to cool. Chop them finely in a food processor and blend with the bread crumbs, garlic and mint.

Season lamb racks with salt and pepper; coat with breading mixture. Return the racks to the oven and roast to 120-degree internal temperature. Remove from oven and allow to rest for 10 minutes before cutting.

Photo on page 137

Salad:
- ½ **cup shiitake mushrooms, stems removed, sliced ⅛-inch thick**
- ½ **cup plum tomatoes, peeled, seeded, sliced into ⅛-inch strips**
- ½ **cup fresh string beans, blanched but crisp**
- ½ **cup cucumber, peeled, seeded, cut into ⅛-inch strips**
- 1 **tablespoon vegetable oil**
- 1 **tablespoon rice wine vinegar**
  Salt to taste
  Black pepper to taste

In a heavy 1-quart sauce pot, melt the butter. Lightly sauté garlic and shallots without burning. Add cream and bring to a simmer; reduce by one-fourth. Whip in cheese, mustard and pepper. Add oregano, basil and rosemary. Reserve for service.

In a pot of salted boiling water, using a sieve, dip the salad vegetables into the water for 10 seconds. Shake off excess water. Toss in a bowl with oil, vinegar, salt and pepper.

Arrange vegetables in the center of serving plate. Spoon a tablespoon of sauce at three points of the plate. Slice the lamb rack and arrange on the sauce with the bones pointing toward the center.

Loin of Midwestern Lamb
with Mustard Seed Crust, Curried Carrot and Red Pepper Jus, Ratatouille of Grilled Vegetables
yield 4 servings

1 recipe Ratatouille of Grilled Vegetables (see recipe on page 81)

Lamb:
1 16-ounce lamb loin, fat trimmed, silverskin removed
Salt to taste
Black pepper to taste
1 tablespoon vegetable oil
¼ cup honey mustard
½ cup dry bread crumbs
1 tablespoon mustard seeds, crushed in a blender
1 tablespoon finely sliced fresh chives
2 tablespoons chopped garlic

Sauce:
1 teaspoon vegetable oil
¾ cup diced, seeded red bell peppers, ¼-inch dice
½ cup diced onion, ¼-inch dice
½ cup peeled, diced carrots, ¼-inch dice
1 tablespoon chopped garlic
1 tablespoon Thai red curry paste (can be found in specialty section of grocery store)
3 cups Chicken Stock (see recipe on page 184)
1 can (14 ounces) coconut milk

Favorite flavors from the Mediterranean come together skillfully in this memorable entree that is perfect for a summer dinner party. Eclectic tastes are added through the use of Thai red curry paste in the vegetable-based sauce.

Preheat outdoor grill or heavy bottomed 12-inch sauté pan. Season the lamb loin with salt and pepper, and rub with oil. Sear on grill or in pan for 1 minute on each side and remove. Rub with honey mustard. Combine the bread crumbs, mustard seeds, chives and garlic and blend well. Roll the lamb loin in the crumbs to coat well and reserve.

To make sauce, heat the vegetable oil in a large heavy bottomed sauce pot and add the peppers, onions and carrots. Over low heat, cook until soft but not burned. Add the garlic and red curry paste. Add the chicken stock and simmer until it reduces to 2 cups. Remove the sauce from the heat; add coconut milk to sauce. Put in blender and blend until smooth. Set aside.

Place the lamb loin in a preheated 350-degree oven for 10 minutes or until it reaches an internal temperature of 120-degrees.

Spoon Ratatouille of Grilled Vegetables in a 4-inch diameter ring mold in the center of the serving plate 1-inch deep. Pat the ratatouille with the back of a spoon to ensure it holds its form when you remove the mold. Carefully remove the mold and slice the lamb loin into 20 even slices; arrange five slices on top of each ratatouille ring. Spoon the sauce around the edge of the ratatouille and serve.

Herbed Medallions of Pork
with Dried Tomatoes, Onion and Ale Sauce
yield 4 servings

Pork Marinade:
- 1 tablespoon peeled, chopped fresh garlic
- 1 teaspoon stemmed, chopped fresh rosemary
- 1 teaspoon stemmed, chopped fresh thyme
  Kosher salt to season
- 1 teaspoon cracked black pepper
- 3 tablespoons vegetable oil
- 4 pork loin medallions (5 ounces each), fat removed

Sauce:
- 1 cup dried tomatoes cut in ⅛-inch dice
- 1 cup ale
- 1 tablespoon butter
- 2½ cups julienne cut onions
- 1 tablespoon chopped garlic
- 1 cup Chicken Stock (see recipe on page 184)
- 1 cup heavy whipping cream
- ¼ cup sliced chives, for garnish

From the Horse & Plow Restaurant comes a dish that suggests some of Wisconsin's ethnic heritage. Perfectly seasoned pork medallions are the center of attention in this entree that uses ale to enrich a lovely vegetable-based sauce.

Whisk together garlic, rosemary, thyme, salt, pepper, and oil. Marinate pork in mixture in refrigerator for 24 hours, if possible.

In a 2-quart saucepan, combine dried tomatoes and ale. Bring to simmer and allow to steep. The tomatoes will begin to absorb the ale. Set aside.

Heat a heavy bottomed 12-inch skillet; sear pork medallions until golden brown. Cook in a preheated 350-degree oven for ten minutes, or until pork reaches 140-degree internal temperature. Remove from oven and reserve.

In the same skillet, melt butter, add onions and sauté on medium heat until well browned, stirring often to avoid burning. Add garlic, reserved tomatoes and ale and chicken stock. Simmer to reduce liquid by one-half and add the cream. Continue to reduce the sauce over high heat until it begins to thicken.

To serve, spoon a portion of onions and tomatoes in center of serving plate. Slice pork medallions ¼-inch thick and fan out over the onions and tomatoes. Spoon any extra sauce over the pork and garnish with fresh chives.

Pan Grilled Medallions of Pork
Warm Salad of French Beans,
Cucumbers and Orange Segments,
Poupon Mustard Spa Basil Vinaigrette
yield 4 servings

Marinade:
- 2 cloves garlic
- 1 shallot
- 2 sprigs thyme
- ½ sprig rosemary
- ½ cup vegetable oil
- ½ teaspoon cracked peppercorns
  Kosher salt to taste
- 6 pork medallions (4 ounces each)

Salad:
- ½ pound French green beans (haricot vert)
- 2 cucumbers
- 3 medium tomatoes
- ½ medium Bermuda onion
- 3 oranges
  Salt to season
  Black pepper to season
- 3 leaves red oak lettuce, for garnish
- 1 bunch chives, for garnish
- 2 medium yellow tomatoes, peeled, diced, for garnish

Dijon Vinaigrette:
- 1 large orange
- ¼ cup vegetable oil flavored with herb stems*
- ⅛ cup rice wine vinegar
- 1½ teaspoons honey
- 1 tablespoon dijon mustard
- ¼ cup minced chives
- ½ cup washed stemmed basil, cut into fine strips
- 4 ounces clear raspberry sparkling water

Photo on page 70

This wonderful dish won first place honors for our Executive Chef, Rhys Lewis, in the 1992 National Pork Producer Council's annual competition. When the occasion calls for something special, remember this prize winner.

Peel and chop garlic and shallot. Remove stems from thyme and rosemary; chop. Combine oil, garlic, shallot, thyme, rosemary, peppercorns, and kosher salt. Marinate the pork medallions in mixture in refrigerator for 24 hours.

Stem and blanch green beans; keep warm. Peel cucumbers and tomatoes; seed and cut in julienne. Peel onion and cut julienne. Peel oranges, cut into segments and remove all white membrane and seeds. Set aside.

To make vinaigrette, grate zest (outer orange rind) from orange. Squeeze juice from orange. You should get 2 teaspoons zest and 1 cup juice.

Blend together oil, vinegar, honey, orange zest, juice, and mustard. Just before serving, add chives, basil and sparkling water; blend well.

Remove the pork medallions from the herb oil marinade and shake off excess. Grill in a hot grill pan to desired doneness, and keep warm.

Combine beans, cucumbers, orange, onions, tomatoes, and season with salt and pepper. Place 3 leaves of the red oak lettuce on the plate at three points. Arrange salad in the center of the plate.

Slice the pork medallions into five thin slices and fan out on the salad. Spoon dijon vinaigrette and use the long chive stems as garnish by inserting them into the salad to stand up. Between the red oak lettuce leaves on the plate, put a small amount of the yellow tomatoes as a garnish and serve.

*Chef's Note: To flavor vegetable oil, soak 2 herb stems of your choice in oil and allow to set for 2 days.

Firecracker Barbecue Pork Ribs

yield 4 servings

Barbecue Salt Rub:
1 tablespoon salt
1½ teaspoons ground black pepper
1 tablespoon sugar
1 tablespoon barbecue seasoning powder

Mopping Sauce:
¼ cup strong coffee
1 tablespoon vegetable oil
1 teaspoon packed brown sugar
1 teaspoon liquid smoke
1 teaspoon chili powder
1 teaspoon salt
1 teaspoon Worcestershire sauce
¼ cup ketchup

Pork Ribs:
5 pounds pork ribs
1 recipe Firecracker Barbecue Sauce (see recipe on page 178)

Here's a dish to remember for your next Fourth of July picnic. Good barbecued ribs get better with this coffee-based mopping sauce shared by our chef's staff.

In a small bowl, combine salt, black pepper, sugar and barbecue seasoning powder. Set aside.

In another small bowl, combine coffee, oil, brown sugar, liquid smoke, chili powder, salt, Worcestershire sauce, and ketchup. Mix well. Set aside.

Place the pork ribs in a pot of seasoned water and bring to a boil. Simmer slowly until the ribs are tender, but not falling apart. Remove from the stock and when cooled, rub with Barbecue Salt Rub.

Place ribs on preheated outdoor grill, without open flames and douse any flames that arise. Brush mopping sauce on ribs frequently, cooking for 5 minutes on each side. When the ribs are well colored but not burnt, brush them with the Firecracker Barbecue Sauce and serve.

Pan Grilled Medallions of Veal Loin
Ragu of Smoked Onions and Rosemary Herb Butter
Mushroom and Scallion Wild Rice Blend
yield 4 servings

1 recipe of Ragu of Smoked Onions (see recipe on page 80)
1 recipe of Mushroom and Scallion Wild Rice Blend (see recipe on page 79)

Veal:
8 veal loin medallions (3 ounces each)
  Salt to taste
  Black pepper to taste
2 tablespoons vegetable oil

Rosemary Butter:
1 teaspoon stemmed, finely chopped fresh rosemary (dry cannot be used)
1 teaspoon stemmed, chopped fresh thyme
1 tablespoon minced fresh chives
1 teaspoon chopped fresh garlic
1 teaspoon finely crushed black peppercorns
½ pound lightly salted butter, softened

Simple elegance is difficult to top and this grilled veal entree fits the criteria. A lovely rosemary-enriched butter melts over the slices of veal in its final presentation.

Season veal with salt and pepper and rub with the oil. Grill on a preheated hot dry grill pan in a well-ventilated area or grill outside on an outdoor grill. Cook until the veal is at 130-degree internal temperature, approximately 5-7 minutes. Reserve in a warm place.

In a medium bowl, combine rosemary, thyme, chives, garlic, and peppercorns; mix into the butter; blend well.

This can be stored for future use by placing some of the butter in the center of waxed paper, folding it over and rolling it into a 1-inch diameter tube. The butter can then be chilled and sliced when needed.

Place one-fourth of the Ragu of Smoked Onions on each plate and set a veal medallion on it. Top with ¼-inch slice of the rosemary herb butter and allow it to melt into the meat. Serve with the Mushroom and Scallion Wild Rice Blend and a fresh green vegetable of your choice.

Pepper Crusted Veal Tenderloin
Wilted Spinach, Dried Tomatoes and Black Olives, Madeira Garlic Jus and Wisconsin Parmesan Polenta

yield 4 servings

1 recipe Wisconsin Parmesan Polenta (see Polenta recipe on page 78)

Veal Tenderloin:
   4 veal tenderloins (6 ounces each), drained, patted dry
      Salt to taste
   2 tablespoons vegetable oil
   ¼ cup honey mustard
   2 tablespoons five peppercorn blend, crushed fine

Vegetables:
   2 cups Beef Stock (see recipe on page 183) or bouillon
   ½ cup dried tomatoes, cut in julienne
   2 pounds leaf spinach, stemmed, washed
   1 tablespoon butter
   ¼ cup black olives, pitted, sliced
   2 tablespoons chopped garlic
      Salt to taste
      Black pepper to taste

Sauce:
   1 tablespoon butter
   ¼ cup peeled, finely chopped shallots
   1 teaspoon chopped garlic
   ½ cup Madeira wine
   1 teaspoon lemon zest
   1 tablespoon chopped parsley

Mild, comforting polenta cools the fire from the peppercorn crust of this veal entree. A colorful selection of vegetables adds to the beauty of the dish and the sauce contributes the panache.

Season veal with salt. Pour oil in preheated heavy ovenproof sauté pan; sear veal well, creating an even brown color. Brush with honey mustard and roll lightly in five peppercorn blend.

Place in a preheated 350-degree oven for 5-7 minutes, uncovered. Internal temperature should be 140-degrees. Reserve in a warm place.

Bring stock to boil and pour over dried tomatoes. Allow to steep until tomatoes are soft, about 15 minutes. Drain and reserve both for later use.

Melt butter in a large sauté pan over medium heat. Add the spinach, reserved dried tomatoes, black olives and garlic; toss until spinach wilts. Season with salt and pepper. Drain excess juices.

In the sauté pan used for the veal, melt butter and lightly sauté shallots and garlic; add wine and simmer, stirring constantly until reduced to ¼ cup. Add reserve beef stock to the sauté pan. Simmer until it is reduced to 1 cup. Add the lemon zest and chopped parsley.

Place three shaped polenta pieces in the center of the serving plate. Place a quarter of the spinach mixture in the center of the plate; slice the veal and place ¼-inch slices between the polenta pieces on each plate. Spoon sauce over veal and serve.

Seared Veal Tenderloin
Salad of Spinach and Basil
Sliced Pears and Fresh Wisconsin Parmesan
yield 4 servings

Marinade:
- 4 veal tenderloins (5 ounces each), silverskin removed
- 1 teaspoon stemmed, chopped rosemary
- 1 teaspoon peeled, chopped garlic
- Salt to taste
- 1 teaspoon crushed black peppercorns
- 4 tablespoons vegetable oil (divided)
- 20 cloves unpeeled garlic
- ¼ cup white wine
- ¼ cup Madeira wine

Salad and Vinaigrette:
- ¼ cup olive oil
- 2 tablespoons peeled, chopped shallots
- 1 tablespoon champagne vinegar
- 2 tablespoons minced chives
- 10 ounces fresh spinach, washed, stemmed
- 25 fresh basil leaves, washed, stemmed
- 12 leaves radicchio lettuce, washed
- 2 ripe pears, peeled, sliced into thin wedges
- 1 cup grated Wisconsin Parmesan cheese

Photo on page 66

Everything comes together in this well-chosen ensemble of delicate veal, salad of spinach and basil, sweet pears and nut-like flavor of the Parmesan cheese.

Season veal tenderloin with rosemary, garlic, salt, peppercorns, and 2 tablespoons oil. Refrigerate for 24 hours, if possible.

Preheat an 8-inch sauté pan; add remaining 2 tablespoons oil and brown veal for 2-3 minutes on each side. Finish in a preheated 350-degree oven for 10 minutes or until medium. Allow to cool to room temperature. Reserve pan.

In a separate ovenproof 8-inch sauté pan, place garlic cloves in a 350-degree oven for approximately 10-15 minutes, or until roasted golden brown. Remove from oven. Peel and reserve for garnish.

In the sauté pan used to sear veal, add wines to deglaze the bottom of the pan. Cook 1-2 minutes and pour into a medium mixing bowl.

Add oil, shallots, vinegar and chives to wine. Blend well. Toss in spinach, basil and radicchio.

Arrange salad in center of serving plate. Slice veal into ¼-inch slices and arrange on greens. Tuck pear slices into greens and sprinkle with cheese. Spoon any extra vinaigrette over salad and place 5 cloves of roasted garlic around dish and serve.

Duckling Confit
Corn Relish and Wild Rice Potato Cakes
Recipe on page 95

Wild Rice Potato Cakes

Recipe on page 83

Carpaccio of Beef and Roasted Tomatoes *with Roasted Pepper Purée and Basil Pesto Sauces*
Recipe on page 4

Pan Grilled Mignon of Kohler Pure Lean™ **Beef** *with Grilled Vegetables*
Recipe on page 117

Pine Nut Crusted Rack of Lamb
Wisconsin Gorgonzola Herb Cream,
Warm Salad of French Beans, and Potato and Pear Flan

Recipe on page 125

Potato and Pear Flan

Recipe on page 85

Passion Fruit Sorbet in Tulip Cup
with Seasonal Fresh Berries

Recipe on page 153

Swedish Apple Cake

Recipe on page 150

clockwise from top

Mint Chocolate Truffles

Recipe on page 166

Dagobert Chocolate Truffle Cake

Recipe on page 145

Desserts

Dagobert Chocolate Truffle Cake

yield 12 servings

Sponge Cake:
- 4 tablespoons unsalted butter, clarified*
- 1 teaspoon vanilla extract
- ½ cup plus 1 tablespoon sifted cake flour
- ⅓ cup plus 1 tablespoon sifted unsweetened cocoa powder
- 4 large eggs
- ⅔ cup sugar

Syrup:
- 1 cup granulated sugar
- ⅓ cup water
- 2 tablespoons Grand Gala or other orange-flavored liqueur

Ganache:
- ½ cup heavy whipping cream
- 1⅞ cups (15 ounces) milk
- 1¾ pounds semisweet chocolate, chopped
- 6 ounces unsalted butter, softened

A chocolate lover's dream-come-true that is served each December at The American Club's "In Celebration of Chocolate" extravaganza. Now you can recreate this luscious dessert at home.

Prepare 9-inch round cake pan by lining bottom of pan with parchment paper cut to fit bottom. Spray all of cake pan with vegetable oil spray.

*To make clarified butter, melt 5 tablespoons butter in small saucepan over low heat. When completely melted, remove from heat, let stand for about 5 minutes allowing the milk solids to settle to the bottom. Skim the foamy white butter from the top; discard. Spoon off the clear yellow liquid and reserve—this is clarified butter. Set aside. Discard the milk solids on the bottom of the pan. You should have approximately 4 tablespoons clarified butter for this recipe.

Combine hot clarified butter and vanilla in small bowl; keep warm. Sift flour and cocoa twice. In a large heatproof mixing bowl, whisk eggs and sugar. Place bowl in saucepan over barely simmering water. Heat to lukewarm, whisking occasionally. Remove bowl from heat. Beat egg mixture at high speed with electric mixer until it has cooled, tripled in bulk and resembles softly whipped cream.

Sift about one-third of flour mixture over whipped eggs. Fold with spatula, quickly but carefully. Fold in one-half of remaining flour mixture, then the other half.

Fold in hot butter mixture; fold completely. Turn batter into prepared pan. Bake in a preheated 350-degree oven until center of cake springs back when touched gently, approximately 20-25

Photo on page 142

minutes. Cool cake in pan on wire rack before unmolding. Chill cake in refrigerator.

In small heavy saucepan, make syrup by combining sugar and water; bring to boil over medium heat. Stir constantly until sugar is completely dissolved. Remove from heat; chill in refrigerator until cold to the touch, about 1 hour. Stir in liqueur when chilled. Set aside.

In small heavy saucepan, make ganache by bringing cream and milk to boil over medium heat. Add chopped chocolate and stir in gently until melted. Add butter, stir until smooth. Cool until firm at room temperature.

Slice cooled 9-inch sponge cake into 3 layers. Brush each layer with chilled syrup—do not soak. (Reserve any extra syrup for other uses.) Place layer of ganache on top of each layer. Using the remaining ganache, pipe lattice on top using a star tip in a pastry tube.

Bittersweet Chocolate Tart

yield one 9-inch tart

Basic Short Dough:
- 2¼ cups all purpose flour
- 7 tablespoons butter, room temperature
- ¾ cup powdered sugar, sifted
  Pinch of salt
- 2 large eggs, room temperature

Tart Filling:
- ¾ cup heavy whipping cream
- ⅓ cup whole milk
- 7 ounces bittersweet chocolate, grated or finely chopped
- 1 large egg, slightly beaten
  Unsweetened cocoa powder, for garnish (optional)

Reserve your very best bittersweet chocolate for this ethereal dessert. You will be rewarded with a deep velvety chocolate flavor that must be tasted to fully appreciate. Our pastry chefs remind you that with all chocolate desserts, this tart is best served at room temperature or slightly warm.

Put flour on work surface, make a well in the center. Cut butter into small pieces in the well. Work the butter with finger tips until completely softened. Add sugar and salt, mix together, then add the eggs and mix. Gradually draw all of the flour into the mixture.

When thoroughly mixed, knead the dough 2 or 3 times with the palm of the hand until the dough is very smooth. Flatten and store in plastic wrap; refrigerate overnight.

Remove dough from the refrigerator and knead with palm of hand until you feel the coolness of the dough in your hand. Shape dough into a flattened circle and begin to roll dough out on a lightly floured surface, to a size of 11 inches. Roll the dough up on your rolling pin, and place dough on top of tart pan.

To make the rim, fold and bend the pastry to create a ring of double thickness of dough, approximately ¼ inch. This edge should extend out from the *inside* edge of the tart pan. To make an even lip, pinch the dough using the fingertips of one hand under the lip and inside of the ring, and using the thumb of the other hand on top of the lip, rotate the pan as you work to get a uniform thickness.

To blind bake the shell, cut out a piece of waxed paper or parchment paper into a ten-inch circle. Place the circle in the tart pan; fill with uncooked dried beans, i.e. kidney, white, navy beans. Make sure that the beans are filled to the top of the pan. Partially bake in a preheated 350-degree oven for approximately 15 minutes or until only lightly browned. Remove and cool shell. After cooled, remove beans and paper.

To make tart filling, in medium saucepan, combine heavy cream and milk and bring to a simmer over moderate heat. Remove the pan from the heat, add the chocolate, and stir until the chocolate is thoroughly melted and the mixture is well blended. Set aside to cool to lukewarm.

When cooled, add the egg and whisk until thoroughly blended. Pour the batter into the partially baked pastry shell. Place in the center of a preheated 375-degree oven and bake until the filling is slightly firm but still trembling in the center, approximately 12-15 minutes. (Watch carefully, ovens vary and baking times may differ slightly.)

Remove from oven and place on a rack to cool. If desired, dust with unsweetened cocoa powder. Serve warm or at room temperature.

Alsatian Plum Tart

yield one 9-inch tart

Pâté a' Foncer:
2¼ cups flour
½ cup butter, softened
1 large egg
1½ teaspoons sugar
¾ teaspoon salt
¼ cup water

Tart:
2¼ pounds dark plums
½ cup packed brown sugar
½ teaspoon cinnamon

Custard Cream:
1 cup heavy whipping cream
4 large eggs
½ cup sugar
2 tablespoons flour
2 tablespoons Armagnac brandy

If you can find them, use damson plums in this lovely European-style fruit and custard tart. The small, blue plums impart a piquant flavor and bake up the color of burgundy wine.

Place flour on the work surface. Make a well in the center and cut the butter into small pieces into the well.

Add the egg, sugar and salt. Cut these ingredients into the flour a little at a time. When all the ingredients are almost thoroughly mixed together, add the water. Knead the dough with the palm of the hand 2 or 3 times. Wrap and chill for several hours before using.

Roll out chilled pâté a' foncer to fit 9-inch pan. Line the pan, trim and chill.

Quarter and pit the plums, discarding pits. Set aside. Combine the brown sugar and cinnamon and sprinkle half over the bottom of the chilled, lined, tart pan. Arrange the plums, skin side down over the bottom. Sprinkle the remaining sugar mixture over the plums. Bake in a preheated 425-degree oven for approximately 15 minutes.

Meanwhile, to make custard cream, combine whipping cream, eggs, sugar, and flour in a medium mixing bowl. Whip for approximately 5 minutes or until it is extremely fluffy. Add brandy; whip for 10 seconds.

Cover the tart with the light custard cream and bake for 15-20 minutes more. Cool in pan on a cooling rack for 1 hour. Refrigerate until use.

Swedish Apple Cake

yield one 9-inch cake

1⅓ cups zwieback biscuits
8 tablespoons butter (divided)
½ cup sugar plus 1 tablespoon sugar (divided)
2 teaspoons cinnamon
8 large tart apples, about 4 pounds
1 tablespoon lemon juice
1 cup heavy whipping cream, whipped
½ cup toasted sliced almonds (optional)

Perhaps the name is a misnomer since this is truly not a cake. However, it is cake-like in its satisfaction level. We think this easy-to-make apple dessert will become a tradition in any family that likes apple-enhanced treats.

Crush the zwieback. Melt 6 tablespoons butter in a 10-inch diameter skillet over moderate heat. Add zwieback crumbs, ½ cup sugar and cinnamon. Stir until crumbs give off a nice toasty aroma. Set aside.

Peel, core and slice 8 large tart apples. (You should get about 8 cups.) Melt remaining 2 tablespoons butter in a 10-inch diameter skillet, add the remaining 1 tablespoon sugar, lemon juice and apples.

Cover and cook over medium heat, turning frequently with a wide spatula until the fruit is tender when pierced, about 10 minutes.

In a 9-inch square pan, layer crumbs and apples (you should have 2 to 3 layers of each); chill overnight. Serve with whipped cream and toasted sliced almonds.

Photo on page 139

Apple & Blackberry Crumble

yield 8 servings

Filling:
- 3 pounds medium tart apples
- 1 pint blackberries
- ½ to 1 cup granulated sugar, depending on taste
- 2 tablespoons flour
- 4 tablespoons butter, melted

Topping:
- 3¾ cups flour
- 1 cup butter, room temperature
- ⅔ cup granulated sugar
- Powdered sugar, optional

Creme Anglaise:
- 2 cups heavy whipping cream
- 7 large egg yolks
- ⅔ cup sugar

Homespun and satisfying, this multiple fruit-flavored crumble is food in pure comfort form. Golden Delicious apples and blackberries produce an earthy, wine-like flavor. For the perfect topping, serve it as our chefs suggest, with cold Creme Anglaise (soft custard).

Peel and core apples; cut in ¼-inch wedges. In large mixing bowl, combine apples and blackberries. Set aside.

In small bowl, mix granulated sugar, flour and melted butter together. Combine with fruit and mix to coat.

To make topping, in large mixing bowl, mix together flour, butter and ⅔ cup granulated sugar; mix until large crumbs form.

Place fruit mixture into 3-quart casserole dish; smooth top. Cover evenly with crumble topping. Bake in a preheated 400-degree oven until rich golden brown and bubbly, approximately 1 hour.

To make Creme Anglaise, in heavy non-aluminum* medium size sauce pan, bring heavy cream just to a boil, over medium heat. Set aside.

In a separate bowl, combine eggs and sugar, stirring constantly. Pour a little hot cream (about ¼ cup) in the egg and sugar mixture to warm eggs. Whisk until blended.

Pour all of egg mixture into boiled cream, stirring vigorously. Place over medium heat, stirring constantly until thickened, about 12 minutes. Remove saucepan from heat. Place inside container of ice water. Chill. Refrigerate, covered, until use.

To serve, dust crumble with powdered sugar (optional) and top with cold Creme Anglaise.

*Chef's Note: Do not use aluminum pans; it will turn the mixture green.

Bourbon Caramel Apple Gratin

yield 6 servings

Pastry Cream:
- 1 cup milk
- 2 large eggs
- ½ cup granulated sugar
- ¼ cup cornstarch
- ¼ cup butter, room temperature
- ¾ cup plus 2 tablespoons heavy whipping cream
- ⅛ cup bourbon

Caramelized Apple Slices:
- 9 large tart apples (4 pounds) (Granny Smith, Golden Delicious or Baldwin)
- 1 cup sugar
- 2 tablespoons superfine sugar
- 1 teaspoon cinnamon
- Mint sprig, for garnish

We doubt that anyone can resist the intrinsic tastes of this dessert. Try this delightfully distinctive dessert at least once when fresh apples are in season. You will never forget the exquisite marriage of flavors.

In small heavy saucepan, heat milk just to boiling. Set aside. In a separate bowl with electric mixer, cream eggs and sugar together to form a thick ribbon; add the cornstarch just to blend. Whisk ¼ cup of the hot milk into the egg and sugar mixture to thin. Add egg mixture to the hot milk in sauce pan. Whisk continuously and bring back to the boil. Continue to whisk, cook and boil for 1 minute.

Remove from the heat and whisk in the butter until incorporated. Chill. When cold, whip the mixture until smooth. Add the heavy whipping cream until a thick pouring cream is achieved. Flavor to taste with the bourbon. Set aside.

Peel and core apples; slice ⅛-inch thick. Place the sugar in a large frying pan over medium high heat, stir constantly until sugar liquifies and turns a deep mahogany color, about 5-10 minutes. Do not allow to smoke. Just as it is turning color, add the apples all at once and stir. Cook until apples are soft and tender. Reserve 18 apple slices for garnish.

Place ⅙ serving of the apples in the middle of dessert plate. Pour ⅙ of cream over the apples until apples are covered completely. Combine superfine sugar and cinnamon; sprinkle over the cream. Place under broiler until sugar is caramelized and sauce begins to bubble. Garnish each serving with reserved apple slices and a sprig of mint, placed at one side.

Passion Fruit Sorbet in Tulip Cup
with Seasonal Fresh Berries
yield 10-12 servings

Sorbet:
- 15 ripe passion fruit
- 2 cups water
- 1 cup plus 2 tablespoons sugar
- ⅔ cup light corn syrup
- ¼ cup fresh lemon juice, strained

Tulip Cup:
- ½ cup butter, melted
- ¾ cup sugar
- ½ cup light corn syrup
- 1 cup flour
- ½ teaspoon ground ginger

Raspberry Purée:
- 1 cup water
- ½ cup plus 1 tablespoon sugar
- ⅓ cup light corn syrup
- 1 pint raspberries

Garnish:
- 1 pint raspberries
- 1 pint blueberries
- 1 pint strawberries, stemmed
- 1 pint blackberries
- Powdered sugar, optional
- Fresh mint sprigs

This sorbet has a refreshing tartness, the tulip cup and sauce adds the sweetness. You will find the presentation is elegant and pleasing to the eye.

Scoop pulp from halved passion fruit, and purée pulp until smooth in bowl of food processor or blender. (You should get 2 cups of purée.)

In a small saucepan, bring water to a boil. Add sugar and stir until dissolved. Remove from heat. Add corn syrup and chill. Add lemon juice and passion fruit purée. Process in ice cream maker according to manufacturer's directions until firm. Reserve, tightly covered in freezer for service.

In a medium bowl, combine butter, sugar and corn syrup and stir until dissolved. Add flour and ginger and mix until smooth. Using 2 tablespoons of batter for each, spoon three circles (they will be approximately 1½-2-inches in diameter), three inches apart on a greased and floured 16x14-inch cookie sheet.

Bake at 350-degrees, approximately 12 minutes or until golden brown. Remove from oven and let stand about 1 minute. Remove pastry circles from pan with a spatula and drape over inverted soup cups until cool.* Repeat process until you have made twelve tulip cups.

In a small saucepan, bring water for Raspberry Purée to a boil. Add sugar and stir until dissolved. Add corn syrup and chill. Reserve.

In food processor or blender, purée raspberries. Strain and stir in ¼ cup of reserved water/sugar mixture; you can add up to ½ cup to thicken to desired consistency.

Photo on page 138

To serve, spoon raspberry purée on dessert plate. Dust tulip cup with powdered sugar and place in center of plate. Scoop passion fruit sorbet in center of tulip cup. Artfully arrange berries around sorbet and garnish with fresh mint.

*Chef's Note: If circle hardens before you have a chance to put it on the soup cup, place in oven for a few seconds to soften so you can place it on the soup cup. Can be stored in a plastic bag at room temperature for up to one week.

Custard Bread Pudding
with Caramel Sauce
yield 12 servings

Bread Pudding:
- 3 cups whole milk
- 5 large eggs
- 1 large egg yolk
- ¾ cup sugar
- 2 teaspoons vanilla
- 5 heaping cups cubed white bread crusts, croissants and/or Danish

Caramel Sauce:
- 1 cup sugar
- 2 cups heavy whipping cream

This is one of our most requested dessert recipes at The American Club. The fragrance of this classic American baked pudding brings back comforting childhood memories of grandma's kitchen. Renew this time-honored tradition today in your own kitchen.

In medium saucepan, heat milk until scalded (180 degrees). Set aside. In large bowl, beat eggs, egg yolk and sugar vigorously for 30 seconds. Add vanilla. Slowly add hot milk to egg mixture, beating slowly at the same time.

Place bread cubes in a 1½ quart glass baking dish. Pour the custard mixture over bread cubes; mix to facilitate absorption. Place baking dish in larger diameter pan. Pour lukewarm water in larger pan until water comes up ⅔ of sides of 1½ quart dish. Bake in a preheated 350-degree oven for approximately 45 minutes or until set.

To make caramel sauce, put the sugar in a deep sauce pan. Stir constantly on medium high heat until sugar liquifies and turns mahogany brown. Immediately add the heavy cream* and stir until all the sugar is dissolved. Cool slightly and serve with the Custard Bread Pudding.

*Chef's Note: When adding heavy cream to the sugar, be careful, as the cream will cause the melted sugar to boil up. The sugar will also become hard again but keep stirring! It will dissolve.

Cafe Calvert Creme Brulee

yield 8 servings

2 cups half & half
2 cups heavy whipping cream
8 large egg yolks
1 cup plus 1 tablespoon
  granulated sugar
⅛ cup coffee extract
¼ cup calvados (French Apple
  Brandy)
  Superfine sugar (optional),
  for garnish

Who would believe that coffee and apple brandy would merge in such a truly delightful way. Use a good quality calvados for best results. A winter time favorite, this dessert should be enjoyed in front of a crackling fireplace.

In a medium saucepan, combine half & half and cream. Bring just to a boil and remove from the heat. Set aside. Combine egg yolks and sugar, mixing just to combine. (Do not over mix!!) Gradually combine the egg mixture with cream mixture. Add coffee extract and calvados.

Place in eight porcelain custard cups in large baking pan. Fill pan with hot water to ½ inch below custard cup rims. Bake in a preheated 350-degree oven, approximately 50-55 minutes or until spongy. Chill.

For those who want to be daring, lightly dust with superfine sugar and caramelize using a propane torch just before serving.

Chocolate Terrine
yield 6 servings

Terrine:
- ½ pound butter, room temperature
- 1 cup sugar
- 3 large eggs*
- ⅔ cup unsweetened cocoa
- 2 teaspoons vanilla
- 6 tablespoons heavy whipping cream, unwhipped
- ½ cup toasted pecans, optional
  Shaved chocolate, for garnish, optional
  Strawberries, for garnish, optional

Chantilly Cream:
- ¾ cup heavy whipping cream
- ⅛ teaspoon cream of tartar
- 2 tablespoons powdered sugar
- 1½ teaspoons almond flavored liqueur

Chocolate in ambrosial form—this frozen, make-ahead dessert incorporates our favorite flavors of butter, cocoa, whipping cream and toasted pecans in a ready-to-slice terrine. A perennial favorite from the clubhouse restaurant at Blackwolf Run that is rich—and oh, so smooth.

In large mixing bowl with an electric mixer, cream butter and sugar until light and fluffy, about 3 minutes.

In a separate small bowl, whip eggs until smooth. Add the whipped eggs *slowly* to the creamed mixture; mix until smooth. Add cocoa and vanilla, then slowly add unwhipped, whipping cream and toasted pecans.

Line a 8½x4½x2½-inch loaf pan with plastic wrap, allowing enough plastic wrap to overhang.

Spoon the terrine into the prepared pan. Fold excess wrap over terrine and press gently to pack it down. Wrap entire pan well with plastic wrap or aluminum foil and freeze. For best results, freeze overnight. (This terrine may be frozen up to one year.)

When ready for use, take out of freezer; thaw for approximately 1 hour.

Meanwhile, make Chantilly Cream. In a medium size bowl with an electric mixer, whip the cream and cream of tartar, until it starts to stiffen. Add sugar and liqueur, whip until it forms stiff peaks.

For serving, slice terrine with a warm knife, place on serving plate and top with Chantilly Cream. You may garnish with shaved chocolate or fanned strawberries.

*Chef's Note: If raw eggs are a concern to you, you may use an egg substitute.

Tiramisu

yield 6 servings

Zabaglione Cream:
- 1/3 cup almond marsala
- 6 large egg yolks
- 1 teaspoon vanilla
- 1/3 cup sugar

Simple Syrup:
- 1/3 cup brewed espresso
- 1/4 cup sugar
- 1/4 cup coffee-flavored liqueur

Cake Mixture:
- 1 pound mascarpone cheese, softened
- 1 10¾ ounce pound cake, thawed, available in your grocer's freezer section
- 1 tablespoon ground espresso coffee, for garnish
  Biscotti cookies, crushed, for garnish

Many of you have enjoyed this traditional dessert from Cucina, our Italian restaurant at the Shops at Woodlake. Tiramisu, translated from Italian, means "lift me up." Its rich flavor blend of almond, espresso and mascarpone cheese will not only lift you up but leave a lasting impression on your taste buds.

Fill a 5 quart dutch oven half full of water; bring to a boil.

In a very large mixing bowl, whisk together the almond marsala, egg yolks and vanilla; whip in the 1/3 cup sugar. Place the bowl over the dutch oven of boiling water, and start whisking egg yolk mixture. Spin the bowl and whip evenly to prevent lumping, until thick and tripled in volume. (The mixture should have the consistency of mayonnaise.) Chill in refrigerator for at least 15 minutes, stirring occasionally.

While mixture is chilling, prepare the simple syrup. In a small saucepan, combine espresso and sugar. Heat until sugar is dissolved. Remove from heat and stir in liqueur; set aside.

In a medium bowl, whip the mascarpone cheese with a whisk until light and fluffy. Combine the mascarpone cheese into the chilled zabaglione cream in a folding motion.

Slice the pound cake in 1-inch slices, then quarter each slice.

Spoon the zabaglione cream into stemmed glasses, fill about one-fourth full. Dip the pound cake quarters in the simple syrup. Place one of the quarters on top of the zabaglione cream in each glass. Repeat the process, finishing with zabaglione cream on top. Sprinkle with espresso and biscotti. Chill until served.*

*Chef's Note: This dessert can be made 3 days ahead of time.

Photo on page 67

White Chocolate Chunk Cookies

yield 4 dozen large cookies

1 cup butter
1 cup packed brown sugar
1 cup granulated sugar
2 large eggs
1 teaspoon vanilla
2 tablespoons Irish Cream liquor
3 cups cake flour
1 teaspoon baking soda
½ teaspoon salt
1 cup chopped walnuts or
  macadamia nuts
1½ cups white chocolate chunks or
  white chocolate chips

The yield on this cookie recipe (4 dozen large cookies) might seem like a lot. But one taste may cause you to think the recipe just might be too small. We think this will become a family favorite at your house.

In a medium bowl with electric mixer, cream the butter and sugars together until light and fluffy. Add eggs, vanilla, and Irish Cream liquor. Set aside. Sift flour, soda and salt; add to butter mixture.

In a separate bowl, combine walnuts and white chocolate chunks then add to mixture, just to blend. Drop by heaping tablespoon onto parchment paper covered cookie sheet, 2-inches apart and bake in a preheated 375-degree oven for approximately 11-13 minutes.

Cool on wire rack.

Photo on page 140

Chocolate Chip Cookies

yield 4 dozen large cookies

1 cup butter (no substitutes)
1 cup packed brown sugar
1 cup granulated sugar
2 large eggs
1 teaspoon vanilla
2 tablespoons brandy (optional)
3 cups cake flour
1 teaspoon baking soda
½ teaspoon salt
1½ cups semisweet chocolate chips
1 cup chopped walnuts

So you think you have the best chocolate chip cookie recipe? Our pastry chefs challenge you to try this version with its flavoring touches and see which your family prefers.

In large bowl with electric mixer, cream the butter and sugars until light and fluffy. Add the eggs one at a time, beating after every addition; beat in vanilla and brandy (if desired). Set aside. Sift together flour, soda and salt and add to butter mixture. Mix until well blended.

In a separate bowl, combine chocolate chips and walnuts. Add to cookie dough, just to blend. Drop by rounded tablespoons onto greased cookie sheets. Bake in a preheated 375-degree oven for approximately 11-13 minutes.

Cool on wire rack.

Photo on page 140

Sable Cookies

yield 4-5 dozen

14 tablespoons butter, room
   temperature
¾ cup powdered sugar, sifted
2 large egg yolks
   Pinch of salt
1 drop vanilla extract
2¼ cups flour
1 large egg
1 tablespoon water

If while tasting these flaky, rich buttery cookies, you begin to hear French accents and sense yourself in a sidewalk cafe along the Cours Mirabeau in Aix-en-Provence, our recipe has worked its magic. These classic French cookies are perfect with coffee or a well-brewed cup of tea.

In a medium bowl with electric mixer, cream butter and sugar until well-blended. Add the egg yolks one at a time; mix until blended. Add the salt and the vanilla extract.

Add the flour and scrape the bowl all over to loosen the butter. Barely mix, just until flour is incorporated. Chill the dough 3 hours or until firm.

Remove from refrigerator and separate dough into 3 pieces; knead until pliable. Roll out on lightly floured surface ⅛-inch thick. Using cookie cutters, cut out shapes and place on *lightly* greased cookie sheet. Chill about 20 minutes.

Beat together egg and water to make an egg wash. Lightly brush egg wash on cookies. Bake in a preheated 350-degree oven approximately 10-15 minutes or until golden brown.

Cool on wire rack.

Photo on page 140

Sandkakor Cookies

yield 3-4 dozen

1 cup butter, room temperature
⅔ cup sugar
1 large egg yolk
¼ teaspoon salt
½ teaspoon ground cardamom
¼ teaspoon baking soda
2 cups unsifted flour
½ cup superfine sugar

A perfect, dainty cookie served each afternoon at tea time in the American Club Library. Cardamom spice enriches the buttery flavor. One will never be enough!

In a medium bowl with electric mixer, cream the butter and sugar until smooth and very, very fluffy. (Volume will increase about one-half again in size.) Stir in egg yolk, salt, ground cardamom, soda, and flour. Blend well.

Shape dough into 1-inch diameter balls. Place about 1 inch apart on ungreased baking sheets. Bake in a preheated 350-degree oven for approximately 15 to 18 minutes until golden.

Remove to wire cooling rack. When completely cool, roll in superfine sugar.

Photo on page 140

Finska Pinnar (Finnish Fingers)

yield 4 dozen

1 cup butter, room temperature
½ cup sugar
1 large egg yolk
¼ teaspoon salt
3 cups unsifted all purpose flour
1 large egg, beaten
¼ cup blanched almonds, chopped
  finely
2 tablespoons sugar

Scandinavians are well-known for their rich butter cookies, especially during the holiday season. Rolled in almonds and sugar, these traditional treats appear in Scandinavian homes at Christmas.

In medium bowl with electric mixer, cream butter and sugar until well-beaten and fluffy. Stir in egg yolk, salt and the flour. Blend well.

Roll dough evenly into ½-inch thick ropes; cut into 2-inch lengths (if mixture does not blend, knead with hand lightly until it comes together). Refrigerate for 10-15 minutes.

Place beaten egg in shallow pan. Combine almonds and sugar in another shallow pan. Roll each length in egg, and then in mixture of nuts and sugar. Place cookies slightly apart on a lightly greased baking sheet. Bake in a preheated 350-degree oven for approximately 15 minutes or until lightly brown.

Photo on page 140

Mormors Syltkakor Cookies

yield 5-6 dozen

Cookies:
  1 cup butter
  ½ cup sugar
  1 large egg yolk
  ¼ teaspoon salt
  2½ cups flour
    Raspberry marmalade or pure
    fruit jam*

Icing:
  2 cups powdered sugar
  2 tablespoons light corn syrup
    Dash of vanilla
  1 tablespoon water (variable)

This is a showcase cookie designed to dazzle in its appearance and flavor. Alternating bands of short (rich) cookie dough and quality raspberry jam, cut at 45-degree angles make this cookie a showstopper. Save this for showers, weddings and special occasions. And yes, it is worth the time it takes to make them!

In a medium bowl with electric mixer, cream butter with sugar until creamy. Stir in egg yolk, salt and flour. Blend well. Shape into ropes ½-inch in diameter and length of an ungreased baking sheet, about 15 inches long. Place on ungreased baking sheet, keeping ropes about 2 inches apart. With your middle finger, press a long groove down the length of each strand. Prick with fork full length of strand.

Bake in a preheated 375-degree oven for approximately 10 minutes. Dough tends to puff up while baking.

Remove cookies from oven. Reform center to make groove again and prick with a fork. Spoon raspberry marmalade or pure fruit jam into the groove.

Return to oven for approximately 5-10 minutes more until dough is firm to touch and light golden in color.

Meanwhile, to make icing, in medium bowl, combine powdered sugar, light corn syrup and vanilla. Add water until mixture has the consistency of melted chocolate.

Drizzle icing with a fork over the cookies. Cool on sheet pans briefly. Cut logs at a 45-degree angle into 1-inch lengths. Transfer to wire racks.

*Chef's Note: Use a pure fruit jam, it holds up better, plus it's healthy for you!

Photo on page 140

Dream Cookies/Drommar

yield 5 dozen

1 cup butter, room temperature
1 cup sugar
1 teaspoon vanilla
2½ cups sifted all purpose flour
½ teaspoon ammonium carbonate, available at a pharmacy (be careful not to inhale)

A pastel, hollow cookie that nevertheless has a crisp outer texture. This is an unusual cookie that will have guests wondering how you made them. You can tell them, if you like.

In medium bowl with electric mixer, cream the butter, sugar and vanilla, until light and fluffy. Add the flour mixed with the ammonium carbonate, blend well.

Shape the dough into small balls, the size of a quarter and place on baking sheet. Bake in a preheated 300-degree oven for 20-25 minutes. Cookies should be very pale and have a cracked surface.

Cool on wire rack.

Photo on page 140

Mint Chocolate Truffles

yield approximately 35 truffles

Truffles:

14 tablespoons heavy whipping cream

10½ ounces semisweet chocolate, finely chopped

7 tablespoons butter, room temperature

2 teaspoons mint extract

Dipping Chocolate:

2 pounds semisweet chocolate, cut into small pieces

1 pound cocoa powder

There may not be a better way to end a memorable meal than with an incredible chocolate truffle. The addition of refreshing mint flavor to our rich truffle adds a perfect flavor fillip.

In a heavy bottom sauce pot, bring the heavy cream to a boil. Place semisweet chocolate and butter in a stainless steel bowl and pour the hot heavy cream over the chocolate and butter; stir gently until the mixture is smooth. Add the mint extract. Refrigerate until the mixture is firm.

Scoop out chocolate mixture and using hands, form small balls, about ¾-inch in diameter. Place them on waxed paper lined cookie sheet and freeze.

Meanwhile, melt 2 pounds semisweet chocolate in top of double boiler over simmering water. Avoid any contact of water with the chocolate—it will cause the chocolate to seize up and lose its natural shine. Stir gently until it is smooth. Dip each truffle into the melted chocolate and remove with a fork; shake off excess chocolate. Roll quickly in the powdered cocoa and set on waxed paper lined cookie sheet. Refrigerate until use. Shake off excess cocoa before serving.

Photo on page 140

For Good Measure

Dried Cranberry Butter

yield 1 pound

1 medium orange
½ cup dried cranberries
2 cups cranberry juice
3 tablespoons sugar
1 pound butter, softened

Craisins, dried cranberries, are one of the newer Wisconsin-grown food products. Their tart, rosey-red chewiness is just right in a flavored butter. Freeze any extras in ready-to-serve amounts to use whenever you serve muffins, breads or a poultry dish.

Grate zest (outer orange layer) from orange; reserve zest.

In a medium saucepan, combine dried cranberries, cranberry juice, reserved orange zest, and sugar. Slowly simmer until cranberries absorb all liquid. Set aside to cool.

In a food processor, chop the cranberry mixture until fine. Add the softened butter, scraping the sides of the food processor down during mixing. Mix until the butter and ingredients are mixed evenly.

Serve the butter in a crock or pipe into stars. Refrigerate.

Ginger Butter

yield 1 pound

½ lemon
1 lime
1 pound butter, softened
2 tablespoons peeled, chopped ginger
1½ teaspoons peeled, chopped garlic
1 tablespoon minced chives
2 tablespoons chopped shallots
  Salt to taste
  Black pepper to taste

Flavored butters add so much to your favorite fish, poultry or fresh vegetable dishes. We wish more cooks would incorporate them into their meals. You can freeze this butter in serving-size amounts for added convenience.

Grate zest (outer yellow rind) from lemon. Squeeze juice from lemon. (You should get 2 tablespoons of juice. Use 1 teaspoon in recipe. Freeze remainder for future use.) Grate zest (outer green rind) from lime. Squeeze juice from lime. (You should get 2 tablespoons juice. Use 1 teaspoon in recipe. Freeze remainder for future use.) Blanch zests in boiling water, finely chop; set aside.

In a large mixing bowl, whip the butter with electric mixer. Add reserved lemon juice and zest, reserved lime juice and zest, ginger, garlic, chives, and shallots. Season with salt and pepper.

Place ginger butter on plastic wrap. Shape and roll so it is 1 inch in diameter. Twist ends tightly. Refrigerate until use.

Basil Pesto

yield 2 cups

1½ pounds fresh basil
1½ cups olive oil
 ¾ cup peeled chopped garlic
 4 anchovy fillets, drained
 ½ cup toasted pine nuts

This sauce will become as necessary in your flavoring file as Worcestershire sauce or soy-based sauces. You can add it to vegetable soup for the Provençale specialty, Pistou, or pasta, pizza, salads or salad dressings.

Wash basil; remove stems. Place basil, olive oil, garlic, anchovies, and toasted pine nuts in a food processor and blend until very smooth.

Store, covered, in refrigerator. Can also be frozen.

Three Tomato Salsa

yield 2 cups

Salsa:

½ cup diced red tomatoes, ¼-inch dice

½ cup diced tomatillo, shucked, washed, ¼-inch dice

½ cup diced yellow tomatoes, ¼-inch dice

½ cup diced red onion, peeled, ¼-inch dice

1 teaspoon peeled, finely chopped garlic

1 tablespoon lemon juice

2 tablespoons lime juice

1 teaspoon packed brown sugar

1 teaspoon seeded, finely chopped jalapeno* pepper

1 tablespoon stemmed chopped cilantro

Serve this multiple-tomato salsa with crisp corn chips or as an accent to any one of your favorite south-of-the-border entrees. Fresh flavors and textures make this memorable.

In a medium stainless steel bowl, combine red tomatoes, tomatillos, yellow tomatoes, red onion, garlic, lemon juice, lime juice, brown sugar, jalapeno pepper, and chopped cilantro. Blend well. Cover and refrigerate until time of serving.

*Chef's Note: When handling hot peppers, avoid touching face and eyes. Wash hands thoroughly with warm, soapy water; rinse well.

Pineapple Salsa

yield 2 cups

¾ cup peeled diced fresh
   pineapple
½ cup finely diced Bermuda
   onion
½ cup finely diced green bell
   pepper
½ cup finely diced red bell
   pepper

Fruit-and-vegetable based salsas are getting equal time with heavier sauces of past food phases. This cool and sweet salsa is the perfect counterpoint to any spicy fish or poultry dish—and it is fat-free.

In a small bowl mix the pineapple, onion, green and red peppers together. Cover and refrigerate.

Dried Tomato Remoulade

yield approximately 3½ cups

½ cup dried tomatoes
1 cup water
1 cup finely chopped dill pickles
½ cup chopped fresh parsley
3 hard-cooked large eggs
6 anchovy fillets
2 cups mayonnaise
¼ cup lemon juice
½ teaspoon salt
¼ teaspoon white pepper

The flavor-intensive sun-dried tomato adds just the right touch to a classic sauce that is terrific with poached fish, crab cakes or shrimp cocktail. This is a wonderful recipe for your dried tomato repertoire.

In a medium bowl, combine dried tomatoes and water. Let hydrate for 30 minutes. Drain; reserve tomatoes.

Grind pickles, parsley, eggs, anchovies, and tomatoes through a meat grinder on fine dice. Blend in mayonnaise, lemon juice and season with salt and pepper.

Store covered in refrigerator.

Italian Cheese Medley

yield 2 cups

½ cup Wisconsin Asiago cheese
½ cup Wisconsin mozzarella cheese
½ cup Wisconsin provolone cheese
½ cup ricotta cheese
1 teaspoon chopped garlic
¼ cup mayonnaise
1 tablespoon Worcestershire sauce
1 teaspoon coarse ground mustard

Our chefs created this four-cheese medley to accompany our Ravioli Fritti appetizer (recipe on page 11). But don't limit this great taste to just one dish. Try it on spaghetti, with lasagna or baked potatoes.

Finely shred Asiago, mozzarella and provolone cheeses and blend together in a medium bowl. Add the ricotta cheese, garlic, mayonnaise, Worcestershire sauce, and mustard. Blend thoroughly.

Cover and chill in refrigerator. This can be made in advance and will keep in the refrigerator for two weeks.

Roasted Tomato Garlic Pizza Sauce

yield 4 cups

3 cups canned diced tomatoes
Salt to taste
Black pepper to taste
1 teaspoon sugar
¼ cup garlic cloves
2 tablespoons olive oil (divided)
2 cups tomato purée
1½ teaspoons dried oregano
1½ teaspoons dried thyme
1 tablespoon chopped fresh basil
1 tablespoon chopped fresh oregano
1 tablespoon chopped fresh thyme

Every pizza begins with a great sauce—or should! Roasting the tomatoes adds special flavors to this chef's special sauce. Add any topping you like after you begin with this basic building component.

Drain juice from diced tomatoes. Season tomatoes with salt, pepper and sugar.

Place tomatoes in a roasting pan; roast in a preheated 300-degree oven for 40 minutes. Stir to prevent burning. Purée tomatoes in food processor.

Toss garlic in 1 tablespoon oil, roast at 350 degrees on a cookie sheet for 10 minutes. Peel and chop garlic.

In a large saucepan, combine roasted tomato purée, garlic, remaining olive oil, tomato puree, and herbs. Bring to simmer; cook for 30 minutes, stirring occasionally. Season to taste.

Unused portion can be frozen.

Champagne Carrot Butter Sauce

yield 1½ cups

1 cup dry white wine
1½ cups peeled, sliced carrots
¼ cup chopped, stemmed fresh
   thyme
1 bay leaf
1 teaspoon peeled, finely
   chopped garlic
½ cup peeled, chopped shallots
½ cup champagne
¼ cup heavy whipping cream
1 pound cold butter
   Salt to taste
   White pepper to taste

Tangy, yet creamy, best describes this sauce that accents any fish or poultry entree. Lovely flavors co-mingle in this delightfully different sauce variation.

Put white wine and carrots in blender; blend until carrots are finely chopped. Pour mixture into a medium sauce pot and bring to a boil. Add thyme, bay leaf, garlic, shallots, and champagne; reduce by half. Add cream; reduce heat and simmer until moisture is almost gone. Whip in cold butter, cut in tablespoons, one at a time; whisk until thoroughly melted. Season to taste. Strain and serve.

Firecracker Barbecue Sauce

yield 4 cups

3 cups chili sauce
1 teaspoon ground black pepper
1 teaspoon ground ginger
1 teaspoon dry mustard
2 teaspoons granulated garlic
¼ cup liquid smoke
¼ cup apple cider vinegar
3 tablespoons packed brown sugar
1 teaspoon chili powder
1½ cups strong coffee
¼ cup Worcestershire sauce
1 teaspoon salt

Every barbecue connoisseur has his or her own secret barbecue sauce. Interesting ingredients add kick to this chef's recipe that is sure to be a hit with your backyard barbecue crowd.

In a large sauce pot, mix together chili sauce, pepper, ginger, mustard, garlic, liquid smoke, vinegar, brown sugar, chili powder, coffee, Worcestershire sauce, and salt. Simmer slowly for 30 minutes.

*Chef's Note: Use this sauce as a dipping sauce or brush on food being barbecued just before serving.

Marinara Sauce

yield 3 cups

1 cup finely chopped onions
1 cup finely chopped green bell
  peppers
½ cup finely chopped celery
2 tablespoons olive oil
1 cup tomato purée
½ cup tomato paste
1 cup chicken stock
4 tablespoons chopped sweet basil
1 tablespoon chopped oregano
1 tablespoon chopped garlic
1 tablespoon sugar
  Salt to taste
  Black pepper to taste

This classic tomato-based sauce speaks Italian in a multitude of tasty ways. Make this sauce and keep it on hand in the refrigerator for the many Italian dishes that require these flavors.

Sauté onions, peppers and celery in olive oil until tender. Mix in tomato purée, tomato paste and chicken stock. Stir in the basil, oregano, garlic, sugar, salt and pepper to taste. Let simmer for ½ hour.

Midwest Muesli

yield 8 cups

½ cup raisins
3 cups wheat flakes
2 cups bran flakes
1 cup dry old-fashioned oats
1 cup sliced almonds
⅓ cup packed brown sugar
  Sliced fresh fruit of your choice
  Nonfat yogurt

Rich in multiple grains and enhanced with raisins and almonds, this European classic has been redesigned for our Wisconsin Room breakfast menu. Team it with fresh fruit and plain nonfat yogurt for a splendid start to your day.

If raisins are clumped together, separate them.

In a large bowl, mix together raisins, wheat flakes, bran flakes, oats, almonds, and brown sugar. Avoid overmixing—it will crush the flakes.*

To serve, put approximately 1 cup of Muesli in a bowl. Top with fresh fruit. Serve yogurt on the side.

*Chef's Note: Muesli can be stored in an airtight container for up to two weeks.

Crunchy Granola

yield 1 gallon

8 cups dry old-fashioned oats
2¼ cups chopped walnuts
2¼ cups whole almonds
⅓ cup packed brown sugar
1⅓ cups sunflower seeds
1 cup sesame seeds
¾ cup raw wheat germ
½ cup safflower oil
½ cup honey

A healthy way to start your day or a good-for-you anytime snack describes our very own granola.

In a large bowl, toss together oats, walnuts, almonds, brown sugar, sunflower seeds, sesame seeds, wheat germ, oil, and honey.

Spray four 11x15-inch cookie sheets with pan spray. Spread mixture out evenly on cookie sheets. Brown granola until crunchy in a preheated 350-degree oven, approximately 8 minutes. Stir often and watch carefully so it doesn't burn.

Store in sealable container at room temperature.

Buttermilk Pancakes

yield 25 4-inch pancakes

2 cups flour
2 tablespoons baking powder
¼ teaspoon salt
3 tablespoons sugar
2 cups buttermilk
2 large eggs
¼ cup vegetable oil

It is difficult to top a good, old-fashioned standard taste. These tender buttermilk pancakes are great plain but even better with a few fresh blueberries sprinkled on each pancake right after you pour them onto the pan or griddle.

In a large bowl, sift together flour, baking powder, salt and sugar. Then add buttermilk, eggs and oil. Blend well.

Drop batter by ¼ cup measure onto hot greased griddle. Cook until lightly browned on both sides. Serve with butter and syrup.

Beef Stock

yield 5 gallons

15 pounds beef bones
6 gallons water
5 pounds onions, peeled,
chopped
2½ pounds celery, chopped
2½ pounds carrots peeled,
chopped
2 bay leaves
1 teaspoon whole black pepper
½ cup chopped fresh thyme

This recipe is a must in every professional chef's stack of recipes. There is no substitute for a rich beef stock. Separate this into useable batches and freeze it in portions for future use.

In a large pot, place the bones in enough boiling water to cover bones. Boil for 10 minutes. Drain and wash with cold water. Add 6 gallons water and bring to a boil, skimming all foam off the top. Add onions, celery, carrots, bay leaves, pepper, and thyme. Simmer for 5 to 6 hours.

Strain stock through a china cap or strainer. Reserve liquid; discard bones and vegetables. Cool stock down quickly. Refrigerate, covered, until ready for use.

Chicken Stock

yield 1 gallon

1 pound chicken bones
1¾ gallons cold water
1 cup coarsely chopped onion
½ cup coarsely chopped carrots
½ cup coarsely chopped celery
1 bay leaf
1 teaspoon salt

Wonderful stocks are the secret to good homemade soups. Once you make your own stock, we doubt if you will ever revert to commercial stocks. Make this when you want something simmering and fragrant in your kitchen.

Rinse chicken bones well with cold water to remove excess blood. Place bones in a large stock pot; add cold water. Bring to boil slowly and skim foam off top periodically as it forms.

When the foam is gone, add onions, carrots, celery, bay leaf, and salt. Simmer gently for 3 hours. Strain. Discard vegetables and bay leaf, leaving just the stock.*

*Chef's Note: Can be frozen for future use.

Brown Chicken Stock

yield 1 gallon

1 pound chicken bones
1¾ gallons cold water
1 cup coarsely chopped onion
½ cup coarsely chopped carrots
½ cup coarsely chopped celery
1 bay leaf
1 teaspoon salt

Pre-browning chicken bones and then deglazing the roasting pan will give you the rich flavor you desire in sauces and soups. Freeze this stock in serving-size amounts for convenience.

Rinse chicken bones well with cold water to remove excess blood. Drain. Loosely pack bones in a roasting pan. Brown bones in a preheated 350-degree oven for about 1 hour or until golden brown. Remove bones from oven. Deglaze roasting pan with a small amount of water. Reserve.

Place bones in a large stock pot; add cold water. Add reserved juices from roasting pan. Bring to boil slowly and skim foam off top periodically as it forms.

When the foam is gone, add onions, carrots, celery, bay leaf, and salt. Simmer gently for 3 hours. Strain. Discard vegetables and bay leaf, leaving just the stock.

Index